Rise of Candidate-Centered Politics

MARTIN P. WATTENBERG

The Rise of Candidate-Centered Politics

Presidential Elections of the 1980s

Harvard University Press
Cambridge, Massachusetts
London, England   1991

Copyright © 1991 by the President and Fellows
   of Harvard College
All rights reserved
Printed in the United States of America
10 9 8 7 6 5 4 3 2 1

This book is printed on acid-free paper, and its binding
materials have been chosen for strength and durability.

Library of Congress Cataloging-in-Publication Data

Wattenberg, Martin P.
   The rise of candidate-centered politics : presidential elections
of the 1980s / Martin P. Wattenberg.
      p.   cm.
   Includes index.
ISBN 0-674-77130-3
   1. Party affiliation—United States.
2. Political parties—United States.
3. Presidents—United States—Election—1980.
4. Presidents—United States—Election—1984.
5. Presidents—United States—Election—1988.
6. United States—Politics and government—1977–.
I. Title.
JK2261.W38   1991
324.973'092—dc20   90-36471
                                              CIP

Preface

This work is in many ways a sequel to my first book, *The Decline of American Political Parties*. Throughout the 1980s, I often considered the question of what impact a less partisan electorate was having on the course of American electoral politics. This book is the result. In it, I seek to offer an interpretation of the presidential elections of the 1980s, as well as to put the candidate-centered nature of these campaigns in historical perspective.

On election night 1980, like many close observers of American electoral politics, I was stunned by Ronald Reagan's unexpectedly large margin of victory. The last-minute shift in Reagan's favor seemed to be a perfect example of the tremendous volatility of public opinion in the candidate-centered age. It also led to the most significant shift in public policy in my lifetime, and left me wanting to take an in-depth look at the factors behind the vote.

In my view, many of the interpretations then being offered seemed to be more appropriate for a partisan than a candidate-centered system. This was most readily apparent in the division of party control of the government, with the Republicans controlling the presidency, and the Democrats the House. As this pattern continued throughout the 1980s, my ideas concerning how the rise of candidate-centered politics had reshaped the electoral process evolved into this work. While this pattern of divided government may well continue for some time to come, the three presidential elections of the 1980s now provide more than enough material to assess new theories of political behavior in the candidate-centered age.

The National Election Study data analyzed in this book were supplied by the Inter-University Consortium for Political and Social Research. I wish to express a special debt of gratitude to all the scholars who worked so hard to design these incredibly comprehensive surveys of the American public. I would also like to thank the members of Public Choice study group at the University of California, Irvine, for their extended discussions of several of the chapters of this book. Although I have not been converted to rational choice theory, I have profited from their insights into the many questions of voter choice discussed here. The anonymous reviewers for Harvard University Press also provided a multitude of useful comments and critiques of the book, which prevented many errors and stimulated many additional thoughts. My editors at Harvard—Aida Donald, Elizabeth Suttell, and Elizabeth Hurwit—were as helpful and thorough as always, and their efforts have clearly improved the manuscript. Throughout, Barbara Atwell and my parents have provided needed moral support for what at times seemed to be an endless project. I am thankful to them and to all who made completion of the book possible.

Irvine, California
1990

Contents

Introduction   1

1   Theories of Voting   13

2   Dealignment in the Electorate   31

3   The Era of Party Disunity   47

4   Presidential Popularity in Decline   66

5   Was There a Mandate?   92

6   Performance-Based Voting   130

7   The Impact of Candidate-Centered Politics   156

Notes   167

Index   179

Tables

2.1   The decline of straight-ticket voting   37

2.2   Key indicators of dealignment, 1952–1988   38

2.3   Respondents neutral toward both parties on like/dislike counts by party identification, 1952–1988   44

3.1   Primary vote total and favorability ratings, 1988   51

3.2   Margins over closest opponent in nominations and general elections (popular votes)   52

3.3   Convention television exposure, 1956–1988   57

3.4   Index of nomination fighting   60

3.5   Standard deviations of candidate feeling thermometer ratings by party, 1984   64

4.1   Evaluations of newly elected presidential candidates   76

4.2   Evaluations of reelected presidential incumbents   77

4.3   Personality evaluations of presidential candidates (and Reagan in 1988)   83

4.4   Voters' comparison of candidates' personal traits   88

5.1   Trends in political ideology   96

5.2   Mean feeling thermometer ratings by ideological self-placement, 1988 and 1972   99

5.3   Republican percentage of the two-party vote by ideology, 1972–1988   100

5.4   Policy attitudes, 1964–1988   102

5.5   Attitudes toward government spending, 1961–1988   108

5.6   Proximity to party leaders on policy scales, 1980–1988   112

5.7   Open-ended policy reasons for voting for or against Reagan and Carter in 1980   118

5.8   Open-ended policy reasons for voting for or against Reagan and Mondale in 1984   119

5.9   Open-ended policy reasons for voting for or against Bush and Dukakis in 1988   121

5.10 Perception and approval of government policy actions during the Reagan years   124

5.11 Open-ended policy reasons for liking or disliking the Reagan administration, 1988   127

6.1   Presidential job approval ratings, 1980–1988   135

6.2   Open-ended performance reasons for voting for or against Reagan and Carter in 1980   137

6.3   Open-ended performance reasons for voting for or against Reagan and Mondale in 1984   138

6.4   Open-ended performance reasons for liking or disliking the Reagan administration, 1988   140

6.5   Regression equations predicting 1984 job approval measures   145

6.6   Regression equation predicting approval of Reagan's handling of the presidency   147

6.7   Regression equations predicting the two-party vote from positive and negative statements about the candidates   150

6.8   Regression equations predicting positive and negative comments about the candidates from policy and performance indices   152

Figures

1.1 Average number of citations per year to *Voting* (Berelson), *The American Voter* (Campbell), and *An Economic Theory of Democracy* (Downs) 19

1.2 Percentage mentioning economic, partisan, and sociological factors in open-ended candidate evaluations 27

3.1 Standard deviation patterns of candidate ratings by index of nomination fighting 62

4.1 Decline in presidential candidate popularity, 1952–1988 (voters only) 72

4.2 Evaluations of winning candidates by voting supporters and opponents 74

The Rise of Candidate-Centered Politics

Introduction

In a political system designed to insulate the government from sudden changes in public opinion, the election of a radically different type of leader, such as Ronald Reagan, and the consequent redirection of public policy constitute a revolutionary development. Scholars of American politics have often asked whether elections really matter. Without a doubt, the elections of the 1980s did. Soon after assuming office, Reagan initiated the most dramatic change in U.S. public policy since 1932, and the subsequent Republican presidential victories of 1984 and 1988 ensured that the change in direction would be more than just a short historical blip.

Rather than signaling the birth of a new Republican era, however, the elections of the 1980s mark a critical threshold in the emergence of the candidate-centered era in American electoral politics. This change in focus from parties to candidates is an important historical trend, which has been gradually taking place over the last several decades.

Most noteworthy about the elections of the 1980s was the degree to which reference points other than political parties became increasingly influential. For example, incumbency was a more significant factor than ever before in the congressional elections of 1986 and 1988, with relatively few close House races and reelection rates of 98 percent. This book examines presidential elections and how candidates for the presidency polarized the electorate to a new degree in 1984 and 1988. This phenomenon can be seen as a change that had been developing over time, as the relevance of the political parties declined. The parties' ability to polarize opinion into rival camps weakened, creating a vacuum in the structure of electoral attitudes. Voters were thus set politically adrift and subject to volatile electoral swings. Like nature, politics abhors a vacuum, and candidates are the most logical force to take the place of parties in this respect. Thus, what Ronald Reagan provided was the strong stimulus necessary to transform the potential for candidate-centered politics into reality.

Understanding how the structure of American electoral politics has been altered by the onset of the candidate-centered age is especially important to interpreting the meaning of the Republican presidential victories of 1980, 1984, and 1988. Much ink was spilled during the 1980s over the question of realignment, as the Republicans pulled nearly even with the Democrats in terms of party identification. Often missing from this discussion of realignment, however, was any recognition of how the nature of partisanship in the electorate has changed over the last several decades.

Party labels, though still intact and enduring for many voters, now often lack the depth and meaning formerly associated with them. While opinions about Reagan were sharply divided, opinions about the parties were not nearly so distinct.[1] In contrast, when great historical figures such as Lincoln, Bryan, or Franklin Roosevelt polarized the electorate, opinions concerning them were quickly incorporated into the party images, thereby polarizing voters along partisan lines as well.

The fact that the Republican victories were more personal

triumphs than party triumphs has important policy consequences. The question has often been posed since the 1980
election of whether the electorate desired a policy change or
rather simply a leadership change. In other words, did the
voters decide what course the government should take or
simply who should steer it? This book adopts the latter viewpoint, based largely on survey data collected by the National
Election Studies.

In the candidate-centered age performance typically out-
weighs policies, and this was surely the case during the presidential elections of the 1980s. Reagan won in 1980 chiefly
because Jimmy Carter was widely perceived as a failed president in terms of results, and was reelected in 1984 because he
was seen to have succeeded where Carter had failed. Similarly, Bush managed to turn the 1988 election into a referendum on peace and prosperity during the Reagan years. Thus,
one might say that the 1980 election was Carter's loss, the
1984 election Reagan's first victory, and the 1988 election his
second.

This is not to say that Reagan's extremism had little effect
on the shape of voter attitudes. In fact, one of the major
findings of this book is that Reagan polarized the electorate
to a much greater degree than any candidate in the three and
a half decades of electoral history now covered by academic
survey research. It is noteworthy that the conventional wisdom of political science has long been that polarizing candidates cannot win elections, as it takes a consensus-building
approach to attain the popularity necessary to win an American election. Indeed, data from open-ended questions regarding the candidates reveal that Reagan was actually *less*
popular in both 1980 and 1984 than any of his recent predecessors in the White House. In particular, the policy questions that most polarized the electorate proved to be a distinctly negative element in Reagan's public image. It was the

more consensual questions of presidential performance—
that is, of results—which decided the elections of the 1980s
in favor of the Republicans.

The Reagan Revolution: Controversy and Accomplishments

The degree to which Reagan did or did not have a policy
mandate was a matter of great controversy from the outset.
Because of the scope and magnitude of Reagan's proposed
policy changes, the mandate question received more space in
the popular press in 1980 than ever before. Headlines such as
"Reagan Buoyed by National Swing to the Right" (*New York
Times*, November 6, 1980) undoubtedly aided the Reagan administration's claim that the election reflected popular preferences for a more conservative government. As Lester Salamon and Alan Abramson wrote in the Urban Institute's
highly acclaimed study of Reagan's first term, "Perhaps the
single most important advantage that the Reagan Administration enjoyed going into its first year was the widespread
impression that it had won a substantial mandate from the
voters for a bold departure in national policy."[2]

Certainly the new administration did not hesitate to assert
overwhelming popular support for its policies. A representative example is pollster Richard Wirthlin's statement, made
in 1981, that "Reagan won because he, not Carter or Anderson, articulated an approach to governance, reflected an
awareness of the role of leadership in motivating masses of
individuals, and provided a sense of vision about America's
future."[3] Many journalists agreed, such as Anthony Lewis,
who wrote in the *New York Times* that "what happened in the
1980 election reflected a profound and general turn to conservatism in the country."[4] In contrast, most academic observers (including this author) countered some months later that

the available survey data indicated that the outcome was primarily due to dissatisfaction with the Iranian hostage crisis, as well as the high unemployment and inflation rates.[5]

Yet as Stanley Kelley points out in his book *Interpreting Elections*, the early press interpretations of an election unquestionably have the greatest political significance in any such debate: "The press gets there first with the most publicity, and the first impressions of elections tend to endure."[6] Thus, more important than whether the Reagan mandate was myth or reality was the fact that many members of Congress, representing key swing votes, believed in it. As Tip O'Neill said, "The record shows there was no mandate. But Congress thinks there was and it's reacting in that manner."[7] Many members of Congress could hardly ignore the idea of a mandate given their constituents' response to Reagan's television and radio appeals urging people to contact their representatives in support of his program.

Like his recent predecessors in office, Reagan fully appreciated the imperative to move quickly on his policies, while Congress might still be cooperative and before his "honeymoon" with the public and the press elapsed. Similarly, Lyndon Johnson's hurried activity to push his program in 1965 was seen by many as due to "an intense anxiety that his popular mandate might be swiftly eroded."[8] As Johnson himself said in January 1965, explaining why there was no time to waste: "I've never seen a Congress that didn't eventually take the measure of the President it was dealing with."[9]

Unlike Johnson or any other recent president, however, Reagan had a very focused and simply defined agenda of major policy goals. He sought to (1) reduce the rate of growth on social service spending; (2) increase the rate of military spending; and (3) cut federal income taxes by 30 percent over three years. If it can be said that the length and complexity of the Carter administration's agenda brought it to ruin,[10] then just the opposite was the case for the Reagan administration. Having a clear and limited set of priorities his first year in office proved to be a major advantage for Reagan in dealing with Congress.

What made the Reagan agenda unique in twentieth-century history, though, was that it called for a fundamental restructuring of federal policies without at the same time proposing a myriad of new programs. The Reagan years mark the longest period during which no major domestic spending programs have been proposed since the days of Herbert Hoover. To Reagan the federal government was more of a problem than a mechanism for solutions on domestic issues.

As a consequence, his budgetary proposals called for the abolition of many discretionary grant programs as well as for spending restrictions and cuts in social insurance programs. Had Congress passed all of what Reagan asked for, federal spending on social services would have been reduced roughly 20 percent during his first term. In the end, the cuts amounted to only about 10 percent—a major change in the course of public policy by any standard.[11]

Yet it would be misleading to say that Reagan succeeded in cutting the growth of federal spending; rather, he significantly redirected it from social services to the military. While spending on social welfare was being curtailed, real defense outlays were being increased by 7 percent a year. These opposite trends resulted in an increase in defense spending from 26 percent of the federal budget in FY 1981 to 32 percent in FY 1985—the largest such increase ever in peacetime.[12]

A final element of the Reagan policy program was the 1981 tax cut. Although Reagan failed to reduce the overall size of government in terms of expenditures, he was successful in reducing the scope of federal revenue collection. The Reagan tax cuts resulted in a decline in the federal tax burden from 20.8 percent of the gross national product in FY 1981 to 18.7 percent in FY 1985.[13]

All told, the implementation of the Reagan agenda produced the most significant changes in the course of American public policy in half a century. As David Broder wrote at the outset of Reagan's second term, "The achievements of the first term are almost enough in themselves to give Reagan standing as a historically significant president. The policy changes on which he campaigned and was elected in 1980, when ratified and enacted by a Congress under his domination in 1981, provided the basis for a fundamental redirection in American government."[14] Or as Martin Shefter and Benjamin Ginsberg have concluded: "Whether or not there has been an enduring change in American *electoral* politics, we have already witnessed a critical transformation in the politics of *policy making* in the United States."[15]

Mandates and Realignment in the 1980s

From the standpoint of conventional democratic theory a realignment of the electorate should occur prior to the implementation of a major change in policy direction. This kind of critical political change is America's "surrogate for revolution," according to Walter Dean Burnham,[16] and starting a policy revolution before a change in popular opinion has occurred is like putting the cart before the horse. Nevertheless, historians have long noted that the New Deal revolution of the 1930s hardly conforms to the ideal pattern. Unlike Reagan, who clearly outlined what he intended to do if elected, in 1932 Roosevelt gave little inkling of all the programs that he would espouse in office. In fact, he ran on a platform of fiscal austerity—calling for a 25 percent *cut* in the federal budget. Therefore, historical precedent does exist for a major policy revolution occurring without a policy mandate, as this book will argue took place after the 1980 election.

Many scholars have argued that a realignment ratifying a change in policy direction is much more likely to occur. This is known in the literature as retrospective voting and is most commonly traced to the writings of V. O. Key. As Key wrote in *The Responsible Electorate:* "The patterns of the major streams of shifting voters graphically reflect the electorate in its great, and perhaps principal, role as an appraiser of past events, past performance, and past actions. It judges retrospectively; it commands prospectively only insofar as it expresses either approval or disapproval or that which has happened before."[17] According to this line of thinking, the 1980 election outcome had little to do with Reagan's proposals. Voters tend to focus their attention on matters they can be relatively confident about, and average voters find it quite difficult to judge the likely consequences of a challenger's proposals. Even if one believes that voters are capable of making such judgments, these projections will be of less importance when it is readily apparent that the state of the nation is poor. In this situation, people know that they are dissatisfied with the current state of affairs and, despite the uncertainty of the alternative, are willing to take a chance rather than stick it out with a perceived failure.

Therefore, the only way Reagan could have lost the 1980 election would have been to lessen the uncertainty and convince many that he would be a worse president than Carter. If, like Barry Goldwater in 1964, he had suggested that social security contributions be made voluntary or that perhaps we should just lob a nuclear weapon into the men's room of the Kremlin, that might have done it. Reagan managed largely to avoid such major missteps and thereby mounted a credible, though not particularly strong, challenge to a very weak incumbent.

While retrospective voting theories discount the possibilities of a mandate in 1980, they point toward the likelihood of an after-the-fact mandate for the Reagan revolution in 1984 and 1988. To quote Key again: "Voters may reject what they have known; or they may approve what they have known. They are not likely to be attracted in great numbers by promises of the novel or the unknown. Once innovation has occurred they may embrace it, even though they would have, earlier, hesitated to venture forth to welcome it."[18] What Key was indirectly referring to here was how public support for the New Deal developed. Just as the 1936 election is commonly thought to have been a ratification of the New Deal, so it might be expected that in 1984 and 1988 the electorate was endorsing the Reagan revolution. Thus, perhaps more important than the question of whether Reagan was accorded a mandate in 1980 is whether an after-the-fact mandate can be found in the survey data from 1984 and 1988.

Interestingly, there were relatively few claims of a mandate from the Republican side in both 1984 and 1988. For example, James Baker, then Reagan's chief of staff, remarked cautiously that the 1984 election "was a big victory for his philosophy and a victory for him personally, but I'm not sitting here claiming it's a big mandate."[19] Similarly, Richard Cheney, then House Republican Policy Committee chairman, said in 1985, "It would be a mistake to fall into the trap that, because he's so popular as a person, that this automatically translates into support for his policies."[20] The major reason for such caution was the minimal degree of change that occurred on the congressional level. This was of course even more true after 1988, when Democrats actually picked up seats in both the House and the Senate. Although Bush occasionally spoke of having a mandate, he never stipulated what it was for, and his first year in office saw no major attempts to push new initiatives through the Democratic-controlled Congress.

Another major reason for the lack of mandate claims in 1984 and 1988 was the reluctance of both Reagan and Bush to put forward their policy plans for the future. It was Reagan's 1984 strategy to replay the 1980 election as much as possible, and having Jimmy Carter's vice president nominated by the Democrats greatly facilitated this. In his acceptance speech at the Democratic convention, Mondale said, "If Mr. Reagan wants to re-run the 1980 campaign, fine. Let them fight over the past—we're fighting for the American future." Yet Mondale could neither escape from his past ties to the Carter administration nor force Reagan into making specific commitments about the future. All Reagan would allow himself to be pinned down on was what he wouldn't do—raise taxes or cut social security benefits. On matters such as tax reform, which was to become the centerpiece of his 1985 and 1986 policy agenda, he remained unspecific. Following this example, Bush made few specific promises in 1988 other than his famous, "Read my lips—no new taxes." Rather than talking about what he hoped to do, Bush concentrated his campaign on what had been accomplished by the Reagan administration.

Thus the elections of 1984 and 1988 can be labeled "double retrospective elections," in that both sides focused on the recent past of the other.[21] Double retrospective elections have played a historically crucial role in past electoral realignments. The elections of 1896 and 1932 are usually thought to be the critical elections in the two most recent party realignments. Yet often overlooked in the study of electoral history is the importance of the elections following them (1900 and 1936), which can be termed "cementing" elections in that the change established in the previous contest was solidified. In each case the party that had lost support during the critical election firmly opted for continuity in the next election rather than trying to shift away from what had been a disastrous course four years earlier. The Democrats in 1900 reacted to William Jennings Bryan's defeat in 1896 by renominating him. Similarly, in 1936 the Republicans chose Alf Landon, who stood by the policies of Hoover rather than trying to dissociate himself from them. The point is that voters may forgive a party that has gone astray once, but twice in a row may transform short-term change into long-term change. The Democrats' nomination of Carter's vice president in 1984 can thus be seen as an invitation for realignment history to repeat itself. And in 1988 the nomination of Reagan's vice president, George Bush, offered the electorate a chance once again to reaffirm its recent decisions.

By all accounts, the gap between Democrats and Republicans narrowed considerably in both 1984 and 1988.[22] Yet, the impact of realignment in the candidate-centered age has been greatly muted in comparison to the electoral upheavals of the past. In an electorate less motivated by partisanship, realignment is easier to induce but less meaningful once it has happened. If one were to apply the theories of Angus Campbell and his coauthors in *The American Voter* to the survey data of the 1980s, one would expect to find that the change in partisanship has had an effect on party control at all levels of government. Such has not been the case, and as a result other theories of voting—principally economic—have assumed greater status.

An Overview

Many facets of candidate-centered voting in presidential elections of the 1980s are examined in this book. Chapter 1 outlines the various disciplinary theories and how they apply to different electoral eras. Psychological variables, such as party identification, are shown to be at the center of a unified interdisciplinary theory of voting. Therefore, the process of dealignment—as discussed in Chapter 2—has had far reaching effects not only on voting behavior but on the electoral process as well. Nevertheless, the importance of party unity has increased as it has become ever more difficult to achieve. Indeed, the candidate with the most united party has won every presidential election from 1964 to 1988. Chapter 3 examines this phenomenon, labeling these years the "era of party disunity." In this era, a winning candidate need not be very popular but must simply keep his party relatively united while the opposition divides itself.

Candidate-centered politics may dominate the electoral process today, but the candidates have become less and less popular in recent elections, as shown in Chapter 4. In particular, never before had a winning candidate been as unpopular as was Reagan in 1980. Furthermore, contrary to the much discussed "teflon factor," there were many negative judgments that stuck to Reagan's public image in both 1984 and 1988. Many of these negatives concerned his conservative policy stands, as shown in the detailed investigation of the mandate question in Chapter 5. The patterns uncovered in this chapter show scant evidence of any rightward shift in public opinion and demonstrate that the marginal shift in the vote toward Reagan had little to do with his policy positions. Of course there was a strong factor in Reagan's favor, namely, presidential performance. Chapter 6 examines the contrast between voters' policy and performance ratings and analyzes the process by which these contradictory attitudes were primarily resolved in favor of the Republicans. And finally, Chapter 7 discusses the impact of candidate-centered elections on American politics.

O N E

Theories of Voting

The subject of voting is one of the most interdisciplinary topics in all of social science. Political science, the natural home for research on voting behavior, has in fact failed to agree on a central paradigm for the analysis of voting. Instead, it has borrowed repeatedly from three related disciplines for a theoretical framework: sociology, psychology, and economics. This chapter examines the scholarly influence of each on voting behavior research over the past four decades, as the literature has undergone a natural progression from initially focusing on fundamental sociological factors, to mediating psychological ties, and finally to assessing short-term economic variables. This scholarly progression makes eminent sense given the transformation from party to candidate-centered politics.

Classic Studies of American Voting Behavior

Most voting behavior research in the first half of the twentieth century employed the sociological approach. This was largely because the best available data were census data demographics, which could easily be compared to voting patterns. Thus, when the technique of survey research first became available, it was natural that demographic variables were examined first, as their role in shaping voting decisions had already been well established by sociologists. In addition, sociology was the first of the disciplines to embrace survey methodology, which is particularly well suited to the analysis of individual voting behavior.[1]

The pioneers of survey research in sociology were led by Paul Lazarsfeld at Columbia University's Bureau of Applied Social Research. Lazarsfeld, Bernard Bereleson, and Hazel Gaudet set out to understand how voting intentions changed during a campaign by interviewing a panel of voters repeatedly during the 1940 election year.[2] Finding that relatively few voters switched back and forth, they fell back upon previously established demographic patterns of voting to explain their findings. The stability of voting preferences and relative lack of susceptibility to media influence were said to be the result of political predispositions stemming from social status, religion, and place of residence.

The initial negative findings on vote switching reported in their study, *The People's Choice*, led to a more in-depth investigation of the role of demographic characteristics. Bereleson, Lazarsfeld, and William McPhee's classic 1954 work entitled *Voting* laid out a comprehensive sociological model of the vote decision.[3] The bulk of their data, as the authors put it, related "either directly to primary groups or to clusters of them in the social strata."[4] The basic assumption was that voting is as much conditioned by who one is as by what one believes. In other words, sociological variables create common group interests that shape the party coalitions and define images concerning which party is most attuned to the needs of various types of people.

To the authors of *Voting*, understanding the past was essential to interpreting the present. Their major concern was to explore the roots of stability rather than the forces of change from election to election. Therefore, the concepts of political heritage and community were crucial to the analysis. "In a very real sense," Bereleson and his coauthors wrote, "any particular election is a composite of various elections and various political and social events . . . The vote is thus a kind of 'moving average' of reactions to the political past."[5]

Early studies of voting that adopted this approach left much of the vote unexplained, however, and were unable to account for shifts in the vote from year to year. This was shown most clearly in another work published in 1954 entitled *The Voter Decides*.[6] Based on nationwide survey data collected by the University of Michigan's Survey Research Center, the book concluded,

> The experience of the last two presidential elections has shown us . . . that the simple classification of voters into sociological categories does not have the explanatory power that at first appeared. It has been demonstrated that the application of the Lazarsfeld index to the national electorate in 1948 resulted in a prediction of the vote not remarkably better than chance. In 1952, the great shifts in group preferences . . . would have been very difficult to predict on the basis of previous voting records.[7]

These weaknesses in the sociological approach led the Michigan investigators to focus more directly on the calculus of individual behavior, and hence relevant psychological theories. Demographic characteristics were downplayed in *The Voter Decides*, with the emphasis instead being on party attachment and people's orientations toward the issues and the candidates.

As with the Columbia study, the Michigan center's first treatise on voting behavior was followed by a far more elaborate landmark work, which fully explicated the underlying theory of their disciplinary approach. The publication of *The American Voter* in 1960 introduced an explicitly social psychological model of the vote.[8] The focal point of this theory was the mediating role of long-term psychological predispositions—particularly that of party identification. As the authors stated at the outset, "Our hypothesis is that the partisan choice the individual voter makes depends in an immediate sense on the strength and direction of the elements comprising a field of psychological forces, where these elements are interpreted as attitudes toward the perceived objects of national politics."[9]

Although conceding that sociological characteristics are crucial in the development of party identification, the psychological approach argues that partisanship is more than simply a political reflection of a voter's upbringing and current social status. Correlations between demographic factors and the vote provide interesting information, "yet information pitched at a low level of abstraction."[10] The important theoretical addition of the psychological view is its argument that party identification acts to filter individuals' views of the political world, providing them not only with a means for making voting decisions but also with a means for interpreting short-term issues and candidacies. Thus, far more than sociological characteristics, psychological variables bear a direct relationship to the vote, as they are more proximally involved in the decision-making process.

The disciplinary approach that emphasizes the factors most proximal to the vote is economics. Political commentators have long been highly cognizant of the critical role of economic performance in influencing electoral outcomes. In both *Voting* and *The American Voter*, however, such performance assessments were largely ignored, perhaps being too obvious.

Unlike the classic sociological and psychological contributions to the voting behavior literature, the economic perspective was introduced by a theoretical rather than an empirical treatise. This was Anthony Downs's seminal 1957 book entitled *An Economic Theory of Democracy*.[11] Instead of testing classical notions of democratic practice, Downs reformulates them according to modern economic theory's assumptions of rationality. Thus, rather than examining how politically informed the public is, Downs lays out a set of conditions under which it is rational to be informed—devoting an entire chapter to "how rational citizens reduce information costs."[12] Whereas *Voting* and *The American Voter* investigate the social and psychological correlates of nonvoting, *An Economic Theory of Democracy* discusses the causes and effects of rational abstention.

The fundamental axiom of Downs's theory is that citizens act rationally in politics. When it comes to voting, Downs writes, "this axiom implies that each citizen casts his vote for the party he believes will provide him with more benefits than any other."[13] The key to this decision process is the voter's perception of expected utility. "As a result," Downs asserts, "the most important part of a voter's decision is the size of his *current party differential*, i.e., the difference between the utility income he actually received in period t and the one he would have received if the opposition had been in power."[14]

In sum, Downs's theory of voting asserts that citizens make voting decisions in a rational calculating manner, taking into account party promises as well as government performance. The vote is not predetermined by social groupings, nor is political behavior shaped by partisan predispositions. Rather, the voter is seen as an individual actor capable of evaluating every new situation and judging what will be in his or her best interest.

How Scholars "Vote with Citations"

It can therefore be said that the six years from 1954 to 1960 was a truly formative period in American voting behavior research. Three seminal works were published, each of which solidly established a unique disciplinary perspective on the subject of voting. In the three decades since their publication, these works—*Voting, The American Voter,* and *An Economic Theory of Democracy*—have set much of the agenda for scholars of voting behavior.

The level of influence of these three books is demonstrated by the frequency with which they have been cited in scholarly articles. It is often said that students vote with their feet, attending classes with the most appealing reputations. As class sizes grow, so does the professor's influence on campus. Scholars, by contrast, communicate with each other primarily through written rather than oral means. Authors thus "vote with their citations," referring in print to works which have influenced their thinking.

Since 1966 the Social Sciences Citation Index (SSCI) has recorded citations in numerous scholarly journals. Taking the period 1966–1987 as a whole, citations to *An Economic Theory of Democracy* have averaged 74 a year, compared to 72 a year for *The American Voter,* and 31 a year for *Voting.* Yet, as can be seen in Figure 1.1, these overall figures disguise markedly different patterns of citation over time. Both *The American Voter* and *Voting* apparently reached the peak of their influence in the 1970s. By the 1980s the rate of citation for each had fallen approximately 40 percent. In contrast, citations to Downs's *Economic Theory of Democracy* have risen steadily throughout this whole period. In the late 1960s it was cited slightly less often than *Voting* and half as often as *The American Voter;* now it is cited over four times as often as the former and more than twice as often as the latter.

In his 1965 foreword to the paperback edition of *An Economic Theory of Democracy* Stanley Kelley wrote that years from now he would "be surprised if Downs's work is not recognized as the starting point of a highly important devel-

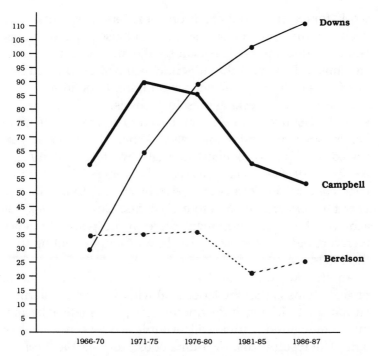

Figure 1.1   Average number of citations per year to *Voting* (Berelson), *The American Voter* (Campbell), and *An Economic Theory of Democracy* (Downs).   *Source:* Social Sciences Citation Index, 1966–1987.

opment in the study of politics."[15] The fact that it took eight years for a paperback edition to appear and that Kelley felt compelled to offer such a prediction indicate that the book was slow to catch the attention of scholars. The citation data from 1966 to 1987 not only verify this impression but also make Kelley's statement seem prophetic.

Differences between theoretical and empirical work no doubt account for some of the variation in the citation patterns shown in Figure 1.1. To begin with, theoretical work is typically far broader in scope. A notable feature of Downs's work, for example, is that it is one of several works that have been instrumental in starting the subdiscipline of public choice. Thus, a possible reason for the increasing number of citations to Downs is that it is now being applied to numerous facets of human behavior in addition to politics.

As a way of checking this hypothesis, the citation data from the last five years were reviewed to determine the number in political science journals.[16] When the scope is narrowed to explicitly political journals, we find that *An Economic Theory of Democracy* has recently averaged 30 citations a year, compared to 22 a year for *The American Voter* and just 6 a year for *Voting*. It is therefore clear that Downs's book has achieved the most prominent place in the political science literature of the three classic works on American voting from the 1950s.

Another key difference between theoretical and empirical presentations is that the latter deal with data from a particular time period. Even if the findings escape the fate of becoming "time-bound," they will eventually be seen as out of date. The result is that over time books such as *The American Voter* and *Voting* will be replaced in citations by more recent demonstrations of similar phenomena. In contrast, theoretical work is not bound to any particular time period. A book such as Downs's can be readily adapted to numerous questions that could never have been imagined at the time of publication. In fact, it is one of the central arguments of this chapter that *An Economic Theory of Democracy* is now much more relevant to the study of American voting behavior than when it was written.

Why Downs Is More Relevant to Voting Behavior in the Candidate-Centered Age

In *The Responsible Electorate* Key outlined a basic model of political behavior known as the "echo chamber" theory. The central idea of this theory was that "the people's verdict can be no more than a selective reflection from among the alternatives and outlooks presented to them."[17] Similarly, scholarly outlooks on voting behavior must reflect how voters present their views during the course of survey interviews. If voters discuss politics in increasingly Downsian terms it should be expected that more analysts will come to rely on Downs's theoretical framework.

As Key argued, the structure of the political debate plays a large role in determining how voters evaluate political issues and make their choices. With the rise of the media and the candidate-centered campaign, much has changed since the 1950s to turn the debate increasingly toward the short-term considerations that Downs focused upon. Whereas candidates were once dependent on the party organizations to get their message out, now they can appeal directly to the electorate via the media. No longer do they have to toe a centrist party line on the issues. They are instead free to craft their own individual appeals tailored specifically to the pressing (as well as the trivial) issues of the day.

Freeing candidates from the parties' control has had the result of turning the focus of the campaign from long-term to short-term issues. Being less tied to the patterns of the past, the American electorate is far more volatile compared to three decades ago, and has grown accustomed to looking directly at the candidates through the mass media. How the candidates have performed in the recent past and what they promise for the not-so-distant future have taken on increased importance. Poll results fluctuate dramatically, as candidates joust with one another over the state of the nation, and the media turn the spotlight from one aspect of the debate to another.

It is probably no accident that as forces which tend to stabilize the vote have declined, academics have come to pay greater attention to economic influences on voting. Downs

portrays the average voter as able to assess questions like
"What have you done for me lately?" better than the voters
portrayed in the Columbia and Michigan studies; and questions of this kind have become increasingly prominent in the
last several elections. It is important to note that although *An
Economic Theory of Democracy* is framed in terms of the strategies which parties employ during elections, the Downsian
model works far better for candidate-centered than for party-
centered politics. Parties, as Downs notes, have a rational
incentive to converge toward the modal point of opinion
when public opinion is distributed in a unimodal fashion—as
in the United States. By doing so, however, they make it
difficult for voters to apply the decision rules that he focuses
upon. As Downs states, "Apparently the more rational political parties are, the less rational voters must be."[18]

A tension thus exists between the rational behavior of parties and voters in the Downsian model. "If either of these is
allowed to dominate the other fully, the model may become
contradictory; i.e., one of the two sets of agents may cease to
behave rationally. Thus if parties succeed in obscuring their
policy decisions in a mist of generalities, and voters are unable to discover what their votes really mean, a *rationality crisis* develops."[19] The tension between parties and voters that Downs identified still exists, but the balance has
changed dramatically. In particular, the degree to which parties cloud the issues (and thereby impede Downsian type
decision making on the part of the voters) has lessened considerably. In several recent elections it has been the parties
rather than the voters that have acted contrary to Downs's
notions of rationality.

It is important to note, however, that the moribund American party machinery had relatively little to do with the clear-
cut choices being offered. Rather, the primary and caucus
voters have promoted noncentrist candidates to prominence.
Numerous studies have found that primary voters are more

ideologically inclined than the general electorate.[20] Furthermore, as Byron Shafer remarks, activists in the nomination
campaign are especially predisposed to "lean away from the
political center due to their lack of concern for a geographi-
cally based electorate" and "dedication to a particular group
or cause as their principal motive for participation."[21]

Party organizations have not consciously ignored Downs's
prescription for electoral success; noncentrist positions have
simply been pushed upon them as part of the tension Downs
spoke of between voters and parties. Voters want meaningful choices, but parties are naturally wary of giving it to them
because of the electoral risk. As control of the nomination
process devolved from the party organizations to the primary
activists and voters, the pendulum shifted in favor of the
alternatives preferred by the latter.

With the institutionalization of the new U.S. nominating
process, it is unlikely that the pendulum will shift back in the
forseeable future. Although the congressional party delegations still contain a fair degree of diversity, in 1988 there was
little divergence of views among each party's presidential
candidates. Howard Baker was the only Republican not
firmly associated with conservative causes who even considered running, and he gave up his remote chance at the presidency to accept the position of White House chief of staff. On
the Democratic side, the creation of a southern regional primary date provided additional incentive for a conservative to
enter the presidential sweepstakes. Nevertheless, such notable conservatives as Senator Sam Nunn stayed on the
sidelines, leaving only the moderate Albert Gore to represent
the Democratic Party's nonliberal faction. The result was that
for the second election in a row the electorate was given a
choice between a clear conservative and a clear liberal—
something that would have seemed inconceivable three decades ago.

In the 1950s Downs's focus on ideology seemed misplaced

to those who studied the average voter, and it quickly became the most criticized aspect of his work. Most notably,
Campbell and his coauthors made the case that survey data
from the Eisenhower-Stevenson contests showed that few
American voters actually employed ideological criteria. First,
they noted, the stable aspects of voting behavior emanate
from "long-term loyalties to the parties rather than ideological commitments." Second, they argued, forces other than
party loyalty "appear almost wholly free of ideological col-
oration." They concluded that there existed an "absence of
overriding public concern to judge the policies of the candidates and their parties against the standards received from
well-elaborated political ideologies."[22]

Yet we must realize that *An Economic Theory* and *The American Voter* approached ideology from rather different func-
tional perspectives. The latter conceived of ideology as the
most sophisticated method of decision making, involving the
collection of much ancillary knowledge. In contrast, the former viewed ideology more as a rational way to reduce information costs. As Downs explains, "With this short cut a voter
can save himself the cost of being informed upon a wide
range of issues."[23]

Downs's emphasis on voting shortcuts fits well with survey results regarding how little attention most people pay to
politics. But his choice of ideology was somewhat questionable given the existence of far easier criteria. As Donald
Stokes noted in one of the first critiques of Downs's book,
many crucial issues do not involve alternative courses of
action. Performance issues, for example, deal merely with
questions of who will do best in reaching universally desired
goals. Stokes writes, "The machinery of the spatial model
will not work if the voters are simply reacting to the association of the parties with some goal or state or symbol that is
positively or negatively valued."[24]

Downs does mention performance considerations, but only as secondary considerations in assessing utility income. In his model, "performance ratings enter a voter's decision-making whenever he thinks both parties have the same platforms and current policies."[25] Rational choice theorists who followed Downs have often reversed priorities, concentrating on the lowered information costs associated with performance as opposed to ideological factors. In short, performance-based voting offers people a rational cognitive shortcut for ensuring that unsuccessful policies are dropped and successful policies continued. Through its analysis, scholars have been able to establish how cycles in the economy affect electoral outcomes, and thereby have extended Downs's increasingly relevant theories.

Changes in Candidate Evaluations since Downs

One indirect method by which the role of the economy in presidential elections can be traced from the 1950s to the 1980s is through voters' responses to open-ended questions about the candidates. Since the National Election Studies began in 1952 each presidential study has asked a representative cross section of the electorate the following set of questions with regard to each of the major candidates:

> Is there anything in particular about _____ that might make you want to vote *for* him? (If so) What is that? Anything else?

> Is there anything in particular about _____ that might make you want to vote *against* him? (If so) What is that? Anything else?

The responses over the ten presidential elections studied to date provide one of the richest data sources available on the factors determining voting decisions. Such questions allow voters to identify what is most important to them about the candidates, regardless of whether such considerations might occur to the designers of the survey. Thus, the data are uniquely suited for comparing economic, sociological, and psychological factors on the vote over time.

Of course, no technique in survey research is without its drawbacks. Some respondents say little or nothing to the open-ended questions—because they are either reluctant to talk openly or unable to express themselves. Others simply repeat what they have heard recently from friends or observed that day on television. And for those who express a number of comments, each one is necessarily treated equally even though some are in fact more important to the individual than others.[26] Nevertheless, there is little reason to suspect that these problems are any different from one survey to another, and hence for time series purposes they remain virtually ideal. It is almost impossible to write closed-ended questions that will be relevant across many campaigns, but with open-ended questions it is up to the respondents themselves to define what is most relevant.

Figure 1.2 shows the trends in the percentage of respondents mentioning economic, partisan, and sociological factors as reasons for voting either for or against a presidential candidate. Economic criteria include comments about government intervention in the economy, which were particularly emphasized by Downs,[27] as well as comments about the economy's health (inflation, unemployment, interest rates, and so on).[28] Partisan comments, which were emphasized by the Michigan center's social psychological approach, consist mostly of remarks indicating that the person likes or dislikes the candidate because of his party affiliation or the general party image.[29] And sociological comments concern which candidate would do best for particular demographic groups, as well as the demographic characteristics of the candidates themselves.[30]

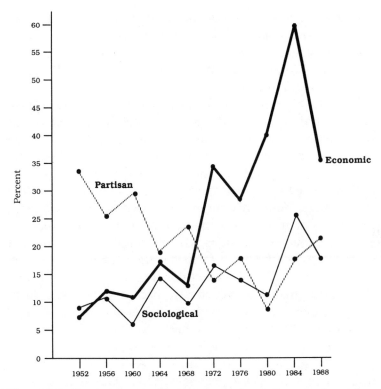

Figure 1.2   Percentage mentioning economic, partisan, and sociological factors in open-ended candidate evaluations.   *Source:* SRC/CPS National Election Studies.

As hypothesized, the open-ended data show a clear increase in the salience of economic evaluations since 1960. In the elections from 1952 to 1960 only about 10 percent of the electorate mentioned an economic factor, compared to an average of 32 percent since 1964, when voters were first faced with a choice between distinct candidates. Most notably, in 1984 this figure reached an all-time high, with nearly 60 percent mentioning an economic issue. The 1984 record can be traced to major two factors: the clearest choice in half a century between a staunch liberal and a staunch conservative; and the frequent comparisons drawn between the results of the Carter-Mondale administration and those of Reagan's first four years in office.

It is probably no coincidence that economic criteria have become more prevalent at the same time that partisan comments have declined. As can also be seen in Figure 1.2, the percentage of the electorate spontaneously evaluating the candidates along partisan lines has dropped from 30 percent in the period up to 1960 to an average of 17 percent in the period since 1964. This pattern fits nicely with the evidence for dealignment that is presented in the following chapter. In the Eisenhower elections, voters typically conceptualized economic issues in terms of which *party* had done the best job in the past.[31] Aside from exceptional times, such as those of 1932, these images remained firm because voters tended to view economic issues through the perceptual screen of partisanship. As short-term economic factors have become less mediated, they have taken on greater significance.

With the decline in the salience of American political parties, one would also expect sociological factors to take on greater importance as alternative political reference points. In 1960 Campbell and his colleagues wrote, "The psychological economy of the individual demands parties as an organizing principle, and if bereft of this, there might be much more straightforward dependence on other groups for guidance."[32] As political parties have lost their relevance over the last several decades, and hence their ability to mobilize the public, interest groups have acquired key resources that have made them more powerful than ever before. For example, direct mail strategies made possible by recent technological advances have enabled groups to better organize potential members, communicate with them about key issues, and raise money for campaigns.

The result has been that presidential candidates have come to rely more on group-based appeals and that voters have reacted accordingly. During the period 1952–1960 an average of just 8.5 percent of those interviewed said they liked or disliked a candidate because of the demographic groups he was for or against. Since 1964 the average has risen to 15.1 percent, with the all-time high of 25.3 percent occurring in 1984, owing to the focus on Mondale's interest group links and concerns about Reagan's ties to the wealthy.

In sum, the decline of long-term party affiliations has opened up possibilities for both short-term economic factors as well as enduring social group attachments to play a far greater part in shaping electoral politics. It should be no surprise, therefore, that Downs's economic model is now being cited more often or that a renaissance of the sociological school is beginning to take place, as witnessed by the recent interest in contextual effects.[33]

The patterns of American voting behavior over the last three decades have, if nothing else, shown that no single theory of voting is best for all time. Rather, each theory is particularly appropriate for a given pattern of behavior. The sociological model fit well when election results showed stability and channels of communication were relatively insular. As the vote started to fluctuate more from year to year, a social psychological theory proved especially useful for separating out sources of stability (partisanship) from those of change (candidates and issues). And as deviations from the "normal vote" became the rule rather than exception, an economic theory emphasizing short-term costs and benefits proved increasingly relevant.

Each of the three major social science approaches thus focuses on different slices of time in the voting decision—from the distant sociological variables, to the mediating psychological ones, to the immediate economic performance factors. Together, a unified theory of voting behavior incorporating all three approaches would look schematically as follows:

DEMOGRAPHIC
CHARACTERISTICS

   lead to →

       PSYCHOLOGICAL
       AFFILIATIONS
       AND BIASES

          which modify/screen →

              CANDIDATE
              PERFORMANCE
              EVALUATIONS
              AND ISSUES

                 which determine →
                     VOTING

As can be seen, psychological variables such as partisanship are at the center of the whole voting process. In an era of declining partisanship, therefore, it is to be expected that short-term economic variables will become more important in guiding political behavior. Without the mediating function of partisanship, voters are more likely to look directly at the candidates, assessing their pluses and minuses. It is thus particularly important to examine the dimensions of this dealignment in depth, a task to which we now turn.

T W O

Dealignment in the Electorate

The term "dealignment" was first used in print by Ronald Inglehart and Avram Hochstein in an article entitled "Alignment and Dealignment of the Electorate in France and the United States."[1] In this 1972 piece Inglehart and Hochstein contrasted the relationship between age and strength of partisan identification in the decaying American system with that in the developing French system.

Two years before Inglehart and Hochstein's article appeared, however, Burnham published his seminal book, *Critical Elections and the Mainsprings of American Politics.*[2] In this work Burnham extensively analyzed what he called the "long-term electoral disaggregation" and "party decomposition" in the United States. While neither of Burnham's terms caught on among political scientists, "dealignment" stuck almost immediately

Whereas realignment involves people changing from one party to another, dealignment concerns people gradually moving away from both. When a car is realigned it is adjusted in one direction or another to improve how it steers. Imagine if the mechanic were to remove the steering mechanism instead of adjusting it. The car would be useless and ineffective. This is what many scholars of elections fear has been happening to the role of parties in the electorate.

What was initially seen as a temporary development opening the way for a new partisan alignment has since come to be widely viewed as an enduring feature of American party politics. Burnham has recently gone so far as to label the dealignment period since 1968 as the sixth American party system. He writes that "in retrospect, the critical realignment that so many people looked for around 1968 actually happened around that date, but in the 'wrong' place. Instead of producing an emergent Republican (or any other) majority, parties themselves were decisively replaced at the margins by the impact of the 'permanent campaign.' "[3] As the old party alignment continues to fade away, Burnham and others believe that a new alignment will find it very difficult to put down roots in the current dealigned era. Any realignment that does occur will be hollow as long as political parties continue to have a weak hold on the electorate. An examination of how partisanship has declined is thus crucial to understanding the development of candidate-centered politics, as well as to interpreting the elections of the 1980s.

Historical Origins of Weak Parties

Americans have traditionally maintained a rather ambivalent attitude toward political parties. The Founding Fathers, viewing parties as necessary evils, initially established them not as long-term organizations, but rather as a short-term means of permanently defeating the opposition faction. Political parties, they believed, were needed only until a national consensus could be attained. Even after the acceptance of regularized opposition parties in the mid-nineteenth century, major steps were taken to weaken their role.

In the spirit of cleaning up government, a number of reforms were instituted, many of which had the effect of forever weakening the parties. In the 1880s the civil service was created, establishing merit criteria for most government jobs. This reform deprived party organizations of the appointment power they had used to reward their friends and financial backers.

Next, ballot reform loosened the hold of partisanship on the electorate. Prior to 1900, the parties each printed a ticket on colored paper that listed all their candidates. Voters would simply take the ticket from their local party leader and drop it in the ballot box. But around the turn of the century the Australian ballot was introduced to discourage the buying of votes. Using this system, the state printed alternative tickets that the voter could check off in secret. Voters could thus now pick and choose from the two tickets, voting for Republicans for some offices and Democrats for others.

Finally, to remove political control from corrupt party bosses, the organization's ultimate power—that of nomination—was taken away. As Boss Tweed of New York said, "I don't care who does the electing, just so long as I do the nominating." Progressive reformers countered with the idea that the cure for the ills of democracy is more democracy. Governor Robert LaFollette of Wisconsin led the charge for primary elections, arguing that such reform would "lessen allegiance to party and increase individual independence, both as to the public official and as to the private citizen."[4] Primary elections spread rapidly in the early twentieth century, making American party organizations the first—and still the only—ones in the world to have the nominating function taken away from them.

It is ironic that parties have been looked upon with such wariness and suspicion in the nation that founded the world's first political party system. Being the first to experiment with democratic political parties has apparently left an indelible imprint on the American ethos. Whereas other countries have consciously adopted a party system in light of experience elsewhere, for the United States parties were a risky adventure in the then uncharted waters of democratic development. From the European perspective, observers such as Philip Williams have been left wondering "how in the 1980s American political parties can be said to have lost power when they hardly ever had any."[5]

Public Attitudes toward Political Parties

Countless survey evidence exists to document Americans' lack of concern with partisanship and the role of political parties in U.S. government. Most pervasive is the belief that one should vote for the candidate, not the party. Even in 1956, when most voters were in fact voting straight tickets, 74 percent of respondents in a Gallup poll agreed with this general belief; by 1968 this figure had risen to 84 percent.[6] In 1986 a survey by Larry Sabato found 92 percent agreeing with the statement, "I always vote for the person who I think is best, regardless of what party they belong to."[7]

On the flip side of the coin, only 14 percent in Sabato's survey agreed with the statement, "I always support the candidates of just one party." This opinion has been shown to be particularly weak among the younger generation. For example, Paul Beck's analysis of the 1973 wave of the Jennings-Neimi socialization study found that 18 percent of the parents felt "it is better to vote a straight ticket than to divide your votes between the parties," compared to a mere 8 percent among their twenty-five-year-old offspring.[8]

With such public opinion data, it can now be said that the principle of putting candidate ahead of party in voting has become a part of the American consensus or creed. One reason is that political parties are not perceived as particularly meaningful in today's political world. For example, in the socialization study mentioned above 86 percent of the parents and 92 percent of their children agreed with the statement, "A candidate's party label does not really tell a person what the candidate's stand will be on the issues." Similarly, the 1980 National Election Study found that 52 percent of the public agreed that "the parties do more to confuse the issues than to provide a clear choice."

The most potentially damaging attitude to the political parties' future, however, is the large percentage of the population which sees little need for parties altogether. Forty-five percent of the 1980 election study sample agreed that "it would be better if, in all elections, we put no party labels on the ballot." Most striking is that 30 percent agreed with the extreme statement, "the truth is we probably don't need political parties anymore." And similarly, 37 percent in Sabato's 1986 survey agreed that "political parties don't really make any difference anymore." Indeed, more people see interest groups as representing their political needs than either of the political parties according to a 1983 Gallup poll.

In stark contrast to political scientists' concerns regarding party decline, the public seems relatively unaware of the parties' plight. A December 1985 *New York Times* poll asked the following question: "Think about how much influence political parties have today. Do they have more influence than they had twenty years ago, less influence, or about the same influence as they had twenty years ago?" The results revealed that 50 percent actually thought the parties have more influence today, compared to 24 percent who said their influence is less, 18 percent who said it is about the same and 8 percent who didn't know. With the public so unaware of the problem of party decline, the task of educating people as to the need for party revitalization takes on even greater difficulty. To make people care once again about political parties will require a public conviction that they can and do fill an important institutional role—a tenet which far too few people currently subscribe to.

The Decline of Party-Line Voting

Analysis of American voting patterns over the course of the twentieth century clearly reveals a steady decline in straight party-line voting. Although sample survey evidence is necessarily limited to the last few decades, one can take a far more extended historical perspective on dealignment by examining aggregate election returns over time. If party loyalties are closely related to the vote, the results for different offices in the same election should closely follow one another. Therefore, if the Democratic presidential candidate does well in a given state, then Democratic candidates for other offices should do similarly well. If voters are casting their ballots on the basis of factors other than party, however, we should find great disparities in the vote won by candidates on the same ticket.

As Burnham has shown, the squared correlation between a state's vote for president and its vote for Senate, House, and governor has declined continuously throughout this century.[9] Table 2.1 displays Burnham's findings from 1900 to 1988, aggregated by decade. In simple terms, at the turn of the century one could almost perfectly predict how a state would vote for Congress and governor by its vote for president. By mid-century a state often followed the same pattern in voting for president as for other offices, but with a fair number of exceptions. In the 1980s, however, knowing a state's presidential vote was virtually no help in predicting its vote for other offices, as the voting patterns were hardly correlated at all.

These patterns are far from academic. They can clearly be

Table 2.1   The decline of straight-ticket voting: R^2 between votes for president and for other offices (non-southern states only)

Decade	President-House	President-Governor	President-Senate
1900s	.85	.82	—
1910s	.54	.75	.84
1920s	.40	.70	.55
1930s	.44	.64	.65
1940s	.65	.75	.82
1950s	.63	.60	.67
1960s	.26	.20	.26
1970s	.16	.31	.04
1980s	.14	.03	.13

Source: The data for each election from 1900 to 1984 can be found in Walter Dean Burnham, "The 1984 Elections and the Future of American Politics," in Ellis Sandoz and Cecil V. Crabb, Jr., eds., *Election 84: Landslide without a Mandate?* (New York: Mentor, 1985), p. 235. I have replicated Burnham's analysis for 1988, with the following results: President-House = .09; President-Senate = .00; and President-Governor = .09.

seen in the unprecedented level of split party control of both the federal and state governments in recent years. As of 1984 only twenty-two states had one party in control of both legislative houses and the governor's office; after the 1988 election this figure dropped to eighteen states. Not since the formation of the Republican Party in the 1850s can one find any comparable split in the history of state party politics. Similarly, for the period between 1981 and 1986 different parties controlled the House and Senate for the first time since 1916. Most visible, of course, has been the division in partisan control of the presidency and the Congress since 1952. By the end of Bush's first term, the same party will have controlled the presidency and the House for just fourteen of the last forty years.

It would be an overstatement, though, to infer that even a majority of voters are now splitting their tickets between major offices. Rather, about a quarter of all voters in 1984 and 1988 split their ticket between presidential and House candidates—roughly twice as many as in the 1950s; these trends are shown in Table 2.2. Some have argued that this behavior is due simply to the nomination of presidential candidates whom many party identifiers could not support. Yet long-

Table 2.2 Key indicators of dealignment, 1952–1988

	1952	1956	1960	1964	1968	1972	1976	1980	1984	1988
Percentage identifying with a party	75	73	75	77	70	64	63	64	64	63
Percentage splitting their ticket between president and House	12	16	14	15	26	30	25	34	25	25
Percentage splitting their ticket between Senate and House	9	10	9	18	22	23	23	31	20	27
Percentage neutral toward both parties	13	16	17	20	17	30	31	37	36	30
Percentage positive toward one party and negative toward the other	50	40	41	38	38	30	31	27	31	34

Source: SRC/CPS National Election Studies.

term increases can also be found in measures that do not involve presidential voting. For example, from 1952 to 1960 the average incidence of ticket splitting between House and Senate candidates was 9 percent; during the 1980s the average was 26 percent.

One might look at this trend optimistically in terms of the future of the parties by noting that in each case about three-quarters of all voters continue to vote for candidates of the same party. But if people voted completely at random, half of all their choices would still appear to be party votes simply by chance. Thus, when a quarter of the electorate splits a ticket between two offices it means that the half-way mark toward voting without regard to party has now been reached. Given the current state of public attitudes concerning the desirability of voting for the candidate rather than the party, there is reason to expect that split-ticket voting may continue to move further toward this threshold.

The Decline of Party Identification and Partisan Images

Accompanying the trend toward greater split-ticket voting has also been a decline in party identification. With the development of the candidate-centered mass media campaign, long-term party loyalties have atrophied substantially. Election studies during the period 1952–1964 consistently found that approximately 75 percent of the electorate identified themselves as either Democrats or Republicans. By 1972 the percentage of respondents identifying with one of the parties had dropped from 77 to 64 percent.

What once appeared to be a continuing downward spiral no longer seems to be such, but instead appears to be a limited period effect in which there was a rapid decline followed by the development of a new, somewhat lower, level of stability. Since 1972 the proportion of the population identifying with one of the parties during presidential elections has held steady at between 63 and 65 percent. As the number of Democratic identifiers declined during the 1980s, the result was that by 1988 more people identified themselves as Independents than anything else.[10]

Yet some have argued that the decline in party identification has been vastly exaggerated, because Independents who report that they think of themselves as "closer" to one of the two parties have still been considered nonpartisans.[11] According to these scholars, the so-called Independent leaners are not an uncommitted and unmobilized bloc, but are instead largely "closet" Democrats and Republicans. Although they may prefer to call themselves Independents rather than Democrats or Republicans, when it comes to their voting behavior in presidential elections they tend to act no different than weak party identifiers. Between 1952 and 1988 the mean defection rate for weak Democrats was 34 percent, compared to 31 percent for Independent Democrats; likewise, weak Republicans defected 15 percent of the time on the average, compared to 14 percent for Independent Republicans. If one therefore considers Independent leaners as simply partisans by another name, then the proportion of the population identifying with a party can hardly be said to have declined at all over the years. As Bruce Keith and his coauthors noted, "Most of the growth in Independents has occurred among the hidden partisans, while the high-level speculations have concerned the genuine Independents, whose increase has been rather modest."[12]

But others, among them Sabato, have argued that "the reluctance of 'leaners' to admit their real party identification in itself is worrisome because it reveals a sea change in attitudes about political parties and their proper role in our society."[13] Even if increased independence has been little more than a movement of partisans into the closet, the question of what is now so attractive about the closet must be addressed. In the 1980 National Election Study respondents who called themselves Independents were handed a list of eleven statements and asked to list which ones described their reasons for identifying themselves as such. The percentage that checked each statement is displayed below.

75%	I decide on the person not the party.
59%	I decide on the issue not the party label.
36%	The parties almost never deliver on their promises.
30%	I support both Democrats and Republicans.
20%	I'm not much interested in politics.
17%	I don't know enough to make a choice.
15%	Neither party stands for what I think is important.
14%	I like both parties about the same.
13%	I'm Independent because of the way I feel about what Jimmy Carter has been doing.
5%	My parents were Independent and I am too.
4%	I dislike both parties.

The primary reasons for independence are thus normative values that one should decide on the person and the issues rather than strictly on the party. These findings support the notion that parties are simply seen as lacking in relevance to the large majority of Independents.

In contrast, there is relatively little evidence for Norman Nie, Sidney Verba, and John Petrocik's "alienation hypothesis," concerning a lack of confidence in the parties.[14] The negative statement most frequently mentioned was that "the parties almost never deliver on their promises," which was checked by slightly over one-third of the Independents. Yet such an opinion could conceivably reflect a perception that parties have become so institutionally irrelevant that they no longer have the *ability* to keep their promises. A far better test of the alienation hypothesis is the statement, "neither party stands for what I think is important," checked by 15 percent of the Independents. And finally, the purest example of dissatisfaction with the parties—"I dislike both parties"—was mentioned by a mere 4 percent. All told, even accepting "inability to deliver on promises" as a negative performance statement, less than 20 percent of the responses indicate a lack of satisfaction with the two political parties.

Indeed, when asked in an open-ended fashion what they like and dislike about the two major political parties, very few Americans have an overall negative evaluation of both parties. Even at the high point of negative feelings toward the parties in 1968, only 10 percent of the public expressed more dislikes than likes about both the Republicans and Democrats. For 1984 and 1988 this figure was down to a miniscule 3 percent—just what is was in 1952 and 1956.

Rather than expressing negative attitudes toward the parties, the dealignment era has been characterized by an increasing proportion of the mass public that is *neutral* toward both parties. The percentage which can be classified as neutral toward both parties has gradually increased from 13 percent in 1952 to an average of 34 percent in the 1980s. Virtually all of these individuals exhibit the following response pattern to the four open-ended questions about the parties in the National Election Studies:

Q. Is there anything in particular that you like about the Democratic Party?

A. No.

Q. Is there anything in particular that you don't like about the Democratic Party?

A. No.

Q. Is there anything in particular that you like about the Republican Party?

A. No.

Q. Is there anything in particular that you don't like about the Republican Party?

A. No.

In Eisenhower and Kennedy's era such a response pattern typically reflected general political ignorance. Most of these people had little to say about the candidates and few voted. For instance, 84 percent of them in the 1960 sample were classified as "no issue content" on Converse's classic measure of levels of conceptualization.[15] In contrast, in 1984 only 44 percent of those who had nothing to say about the parties failed to mention an issue when they were asked about the candidates. In the 1980s such individuals have tuned out the parties but not necessarily the candidates and the issues. Indeed, they are often considered the most important group in American electoral politics—known collectively as the "floating voters."

Compared to the decline of party identification, the rise of neutrality in party images has occurred over a much longer period of time and been a far more pronounced trend. The major reason for this discrepancy is that party identification involves a process of self-labeling and is therefore likely to be more stable than most other political attitudes.[16] But this stability can be seen as a theoretical weakness of the measure as well as a strength. While the label may survive intact from year to year, the meaning associated with it may change considerably over time. If parties have become less relevant to the public in recent decades, then it is to be expected that citizens' opinions about the parties will have weakened— even among those whose party labels remain intact.

The best possible test for this hypothesis is to examine how people have responded to party likes/dislikes questions over time, controlling for party identification. As Table 2.3 shows, the increase in neutrality is evident for all groups—strong partisans, weak partisans, independent leaners, and pure independents. Thus, strength of party identification no longer has the depth of meaning attached to it that it once did. The significance of the rise of neutrality, therefore, is not so much that it explains the decline of party identification as that it indicates that the decline in party relevance is even sharper than the rise in independence would lead us to expect.

Table 2.3 Respondents neutral toward both parties on like/dislike counts by party identification, 1952–1988 (in percents)

	1952	1956	1960	1964	1968	1972	1976	1980	1984	1988
Strong Democrats	5	6	6	8	6	9	9	14	14	16
Strong Republicans	5	10	8	5	8	12	12	18	14	12
Weak Democrats	15	14	15	21	22	29	29	37	37	30
Weak Republicans	14	16	15	27	16	33	34	32	37	33
Independent Democrats	13	11	16	24	15	35	37	48	38	28
Independent Republicans	10	21	12	19	14	35	34	36	41	34
Pure Independents	23	32	49	46	34	53	57	64	70	63

Source: SRC/CPS National Election Studies.
Note: Neutral toward both parties is defined as having an equal number of likes and dislikes about each. Roughly 90 percent of these cases result from respondents' saying they have neither likes nor dislikes about the parties.

. . .

As the candidate-centered age reaches maturity, there is little reason to suspect that these dealigning trends will be substantially reversed. Even the Reagan-Mondale contest of 1984, which pitted a traditional Democrat against the most partisan president in recent memory, did little to undo the dealigned state of the American electorate.

During the early stages of the dealignment many analysts were concerned that parties were on the verge of disappearing from the political scene. As dealignment has progressed, a more realistic view has been that parties will continue to play an important but significantly diminished role in American electoral politics. For example, Leon Epstein writes that "frayed" strikes him as "an apt word for what has happened to party identification during the last three decades . . . The word connotes a wearing that need not mean disintegration or abandonment."[17] He concludes that the parties will "survive and even moderately prosper in a society evidently unreceptive to strong parties and yet unready, and probably unable, to abandon parties altogether."[18]

The data reviewed in this chapter concerning normative attitudes toward the parties indicate that most voters now view parties as a convenience rather than a necessity. Yet, regardless of whether the public recognizes it or not, parties are necessities for structuring the vote. Political scientists have long recognized the indispensable functions performed by parties, and dealignment has only reinforced this view. As Dalton, Flanagan, and Beck write, "Unless elections become purely contests of personalities, parties are likely to continue to play an important role in structuring political choices, even in a purely dealigned and issue-oriented electorate."[19]

The key question is not whether political parties can survive in an atmosphere of dealignment, but rather whether they can still perform many of their key functions in such an atmosphere. If many voters no longer pay attention to party labels, what reason is there for elites to pay more than lip service to the concept of party unity either in campaigns or in governing? When Eisenhower was first nominated in 1952, he told the Republican convention that in order to achieve their aims there must be a "total victory." As he put it, "We must have more Republicans in our state and local offices; more Republican governments in our states; a Republican majority in the United States House of Representatives and in the United States Senate; and, of course, a Republican in the White House." Now candidates rarely utter the name of their party, and the last two elections have seen recriminations from disgruntled congressional leaders, Michel of the House (1984) and Dole of the Senate (1988), regarding the lack of help from the top of the ticket.

THREE

The Era of Party Disunity

Although the role of partisanship in shaping political attitudes has greatly diminished in recent years, unified party support remains crucial to a presidential election victory. Indeed, one of the key features of the candidate-centered age is the increasingly difficult task of unifying a political party in November when the various factions within it have been competing for so long. Internal animosities stirred up by the reformed nomination process are more likely to continue to haunt the nominee in November. These animosities hurt a candidate not only with his own party's voters but with Independents and the opposition party as well. After all, if members of the candidate's own party find fault with their nominee why should those outside the party view him favorably?

Partisan splits have figured prominently in electoral outcomes at various times throughout American history. For example, the Taft-Roosevelt split within the Republican Party in 1912 opened the way for Wilson to win the presidency in that year. Surely the most divisive contest of all was the Democrats' 103-ballot marathon in 1924, which left the Democrats so torn apart that they were not able to mount much of a challenge to Coolidge even with the Republicans' Teapot Dome scandal still fresh in the electorate's mind.

Yet, taking the number of presidential ballots at the conventions as a measure of party unity shows that this was by no means a sure predictor of election outcomes in the pre-television era. From Reconstruction through World War II there were twelve cases in which one party took more ballots than the other to choose its nominee. Of these twelve campaigns, just seven were won by the party that reached its decision quickest.

Party disunity also did not fatally damage the campaigns of Truman in 1948, Eisenhower in 1952, and Kennedy in 1960. Truman was faced by splinter party candidates Thurmond on the right and Wallace on the left, both of whom represented Democratic factions he had alienated. Eisenhower had to resort to credentials challenges at the convention to pry the Republican nomination away from Taft. And Kennedy barely managed to squeeze together a majority of delegates, whereas Nixon ran unopposed on the Republican side. In all three cases, however, the candidate whose party exhibited the most divisiveness at the convention went on to win anyway.

In contrast, *the candidate with the most united party has won every presidential election from 1964 to 1988.* One paradoxical effect of dealignment has been that party unity has taken on greater importance as it has become more difficult to achieve. Thus, I believe that one of the most appropriate labels for party politics in the years since Kennedy's death is the "era of party disunity." This chapter provides evidence for the thesis that a successful campaign now depends on wrapping up the nomination faster and with less lingering bitterness than the opposition.

State-Level Data on Divisive Presidential Primaries

Numerous studies have shown that a divisive state primary adversely affects a nominee's chances of winning the state in the fall. Party activists who invest their efforts in losing campaigns for the nomination are often reluctant to continue their campaign involvement during the general election. For example, Emmett Buell's study of New Hampshire primary activists in 1984 found that about half of the supporters of Mondale's Democratic rivals virtually sat out the November campaign.[1] Thus, just when Mondale needed all the support he could get from his party, he found it difficult to overcome the divisions of the spring's campaign. This phenomenon seems to be primarily due to personal loyalty to the losing candidates rather than to ideological differences. As Walter Stone found in his study of 1980 Iowa activists, nomination preferences in both parties significantly affected participation, *independent of* the effects of ideology, past levels of political activity, and attachment to the party organization.[2]

Throughout the history of presidential primaries, divisive primaries have seriously hurt a party's chances of winning those same states in November.[3] In the most comprehensive study to date, Patrick Kenney and Tom Rice make use of the percentage of the primary vote received by both nominees in each state from 1912 to 1984 to assess the relative effect of divisive primaries.[4] They find that for every percent that one nominee does better than the other in a given state, an additional .07 percent of the vote is gained over what would otherwise be expected in November. The effect is analogous to becoming a favorite son candidate; having done well in the state during the primaries, a nominee naturally begins the general election campaign in that state with the image of a winner—both well known and well liked. In contrast, when a candidate makes a poor showing in a state primary, he starts the general election campaign there with a serious handicap.

To illustrate this effect, Table 3.1 presents exit poll data from selected 1988 primaries in which voters were asked, "Regardless of how you voted today is your opinion of (George Bush/Michael Dukakis) favorable or unfavorable?" For both candidates, the relationship between primary votes and favorability ratings is clear (R > .90). Despite the fact that Bush averaged a much higher percentage of the vote than Dukakis, the two equations predicting positive ratings from the vote are nearly identical. The constant is slightly over 40 percent in both cases, and for every point gained in the primary vote the nominee gains .57 percent in popularity.

Thus in primaries where a candidate does poorly at the ballot box, his approval rating suffers markedly, In states such as Mississippi, Alabama, and Tennessee, for example, Dukakis's single-digit finish left him with meager favorability ratings of under 50 percent among Democrats. Similarly, in states where Dole gave Bush a strong challenge (Missouri, Oklahoma, and Arkansas), positive ratings of Bush were notably fewer than elsewhere in the south. Although primaries are contested by like-minded politicians who should be widely approved of by party members, the zero-sum nature of the electoral process often works to the contrary.

Should one party have a long set of divisive contests and the other none at all, such as in 1984, the impact is particularly marked. Overall, Mondale received about 38 percent of the Democratic primary vote versus 98 percent of the Republican vote for Reagan. Extrapolating from Kenney and Rice's equation, this translates into an additional 4.2 percent (.07 [98 − 38]) of the vote for Reagan in a typical 1984 primary state. In 1988 Bush received 68 percent of the total Republican primary vote compared to 42 percent of the Democratic vote for Dukakis, thereby giving Bush a predicted

Table 3.1 Primary vote total and favorability ratings, 1988

State	Bush[a]		Dukakis[b]	
	% favorable among own partisans	% of primary vote	% favorable among own partisans	% of primary vote
Alabama	82	65	44	8
Arkansas	63	47	53	19
Florida	73	62	67	41
Georgia	71	54	54	16
Louisiana	75	58	50	15
Massachusetts	74	59	72	59
Mississippi	80	66	42	8
Missouri	67	42	50	12
North Carolina	70	45	60	20
Oklahoma	62	37	50	17
Tennessee	75	60	44	3
Texas	77	64	64	33
Virginia	73	53	60	22
Illinois	70	55	60	16
Wisconsin	n.a.	82	73	48
New York	—	—	72	51

Source: New York Times/CBS exit polls, as reported in *Public Opinion*, May/June 1988, pp. 24–25.

a. Bush favorability = $40.9 + .57$ (VOTE) R = .90, t stat = 7.33, std err = .08

b. Dukakis favorability = $43.3 + .57$ (VOTE), R = .93, t stat = 9.88, std err = .06

edge of 1.8 percent in the average primary state over what would normally be expected in November.

Nationwide Data for the Disunity Hypothesis

Whereas several studies have attempted to assess the effect of divisive presidential primaries at the state level, there has been little examination of this phenomenon using national data. With the passage of time since the first successful candidate-centered insurgency by Goldwater, one can now compare data from a dozen national campaigns. And since 1964 the candidate with the least encumbered path to the nomination has proven to be the victor in November. As shown in Table 3.2, the greater the margin a nominee ac-

Table 3.2   Margins over closest opponent in nominations and general elections (popular votes)

Candidate	Nomination margin (%)	General election margin (%)
Bush (1988)	+48.5	+7.8
Reagan (1980)	+37.5	+9.7
Carter (1976)	+23.5	+2.1
Carter (1980)	+14.1	−9.7
Dukakis (1988)	+13.2	−7.8
Ford (1976)	+7.4	−2.1
Mondale (1984)	+1.7	−18.2
Goldwater (1964)[a]	+1.0	−22.5
McGovern (1972)	−0.5	−23.2

Source: Congressional Quarterly, Inc.

a. Based on contested primaries between Goldwater and Rockefeller in New Hampshire, Oregon, and California only.

cumulates over his closest rival in the primaries, the better he does in the general election. Candidates who ran virtually even with their closest challenger throughout the primaries, such as Goldwater, McGovern, and Mondale, ended up on the losing side of landslide elections. In contrast, Carter in 1976 and Reagan in 1980—both of whom far outdistanced their primary rivals—unseated incumbent presidents who faced relatively close nomination contests. Of course, incumbent presidents who were scarcely challenged in the primaries fared best of all.

During the nomination campaign there are four key points where party divisiveness can arise: (1) early primaries; (2) late primaries; (3) the convention; and (4) the vice presidential selection. In the era of party disunity the candidate who locks up his party's nomination quickest, and is therefore able to bypass the problems of the later stages, establishes a great advantage for the fall campaign. In other words, the more partisan dissension a nominee accumulates during these four stages, the less chance he has of actually winning the presidency.

The first stage of party divisiveness occurs in the early primary contests in states like New Hampshire and Illinois. Even a brief series of early challenges, such as by Bush and Anderson against Reagan, can leave a lasting imprint on party unity. Of course, such contests have now become inevitable in races without an incumbent. Even established front-runners, like Reagan in 1980 or Mondale in 1984, faced challenges from half a dozen opponents who hoped they could overcome the uphill odds. The best a party can expect in this situation is to have the nomination decided quickly, with as little bitterness as possible.

A second stage of divisiveness in the nomination process hence occurs if the contests continue through the later primaries, such as California. What *Newsweek* once labeled "caucus fatigue" or "postprimary depression"comes into play at this point. As the article facetiously but insightfully noted in April 1984, this can be defined as "a rare form of exhaustion, usually temporary, known to afflict presidential candidates. Common symptoms include listlessness after victory, a pattern of tactical blunders often blamed on one's staff, a propensity for negative campaigning, and a crippling inability to say anything inspiring about America's future"[5] As the number of candidates is winnowed down to two or three, the press has a greater ability to focus on their particular weaknesses and criticisms of each other. The longer and more wide open the campaign becomes, the more candidates must develop new issues and reasons for people not to vote for their opponents. Intra-party criticism is hardly new in American politics. J. Morgan Kousser's analysis of the rise of primaries in the south around the turn of the century, for instance, shows how it became necessary for candidates "to lambaste their opponents publicly" and to "fabricate issues" in order to attract attention.[6]

The continual backbiting in the nomination process has been greatly exacerbated in recent years by the custom of regular televised debates by the candidates prior to each major primary date. When debates were first introduced at the dawn of the television era, one might say that they showed the characteristics of a kindler, gentler America (to use George Bush's famous phrase). For example, when Stevenson and Kefauver debated prior to the 1956 Florida primary the *New York Times* reported, "The nationally televised 'debate' found the two chief contenders for the Democratic Presidential nomination taking virtually identical positions on almost every issue discussed."[7] Similarly, when Kennedy debated Humphrey on West Virginia television in 1960 the UPI story led with the following introduction: "Sens. Kennedy and Humphrey staged a debate with kid gloves tonight and found little to disagree about except whether Humphrey has a chance to win the Democratic Presidential nomination."[8] Rather than tearing each other down, the two candidates focused on the merits of Democratic Party proposals. Indeed, the Republican national chairman demanded equal time, arguing that the "debate" had enabled the Democrats to advertise their positions. In his view, the joint appearance had "all the sharpness of a duel with bananas," and "a pillow fight between two small boys would have been more controversial."[9]

By the 1980s, party leaders were delighted to see the other party's candidates debating on television. As presidential primaries proliferated and their results became decisive, the incentive for openly criticizing one's opponents increased dramatically. That the kid gloves of the early television era have been dropped is evident in the *New York Times*'s description of the 1984 Atlanta debate, which was "marked by sharp clashes," with Walter Mondale using "every device from wisecracks to condemnation." Other candidates were variously defined as having "attacked," "ridiculed," "ganged up on," "jabbed," and "accused" their opponents.[10]

With so much riding on their public performances, candidates now feel compelled to differentiate themselves as much as possible—even if they have few policy differences. Nelson Polsby points out that Henry Jackson and Morris Udall, for example, were perceived as polar opposites on domestic policy during the 1976 Democratic campaign despite the great similarity in their congressional voting records.[11] Thus the public comes to see more conflict within the party than really exists and is led to doubt whether the party label means anything. In this sense, it is clear that primaries do more than merely display the existing disunity.

Recognizing the dangers of such internal conflicts, Democratic National Chairman Paul Kirk set up a committee of party elders in 1988 to monitor the campaign and to "publicly bring political pressure to bear on any candidate who refuses to be civil."[12] Yet, while the Democratic campaign of 1988 contained nothing as extreme as Gary Hart's 1984 charges that Walter Mondale was the unelectable candidate of the past, Dukakis hardly emerged unscathed from his thirty-nine debate appearances. It was Albert Gore in the New York debate who first introduced the issue of the furlough of Willie Horton—an issue that George Bush would later pick up on. And Jesse Jackson often stated that whereas he wanted to reverse Reaganomics, Dukakis wanted only to "manage" it. He further criticized Dukakis for not preparing a federal budget, for being as "bland" as Bush, and at one point even accused him of being to the right of Reagan on Mozambique.[13]

If these sorts of criticisms continue week after week, the enthusiasm for the front-runner inevitably fades. As Lee Atwater has said, every Tuesday a candidate is "facing two challenges: (a) people saying that this guy is not capable of leading the country, and (b) people saying that not only is he not capable of leading the country, he's not capable of leading this party."[14] The phenomenon of "negative momentum," therefore, often occurs as a candidate nears the point of clinching the nomination.[15] Gerald Ford, for instance, not only still faced opposition at the end of the 1976 primary season but was soundly defeated by Reagan over the last three weeks in Arkansas, Idaho, Nevada, Montana, and of course California. As a result, he limped into the Republican convention with barely enough delegates to win.

Negative momentum at the end of the primary season often leads to a major floor fight at the convention itself. Even a convention fight that seems little more than a last gasp, such as Reagan's in 1976 or Kennedy's in 1980, can cause much damage to party unity. Despite the decline of the convention as a decision-making body, more media coverage is nevertheless focused on it than any other event in the nomination process.[16] It is therefore especially harmful for a nominee to be challenged from within at this highly visible stage, which constitutes our third indicator of nomination divisiveness.

Indeed, the data on convention television exposure in Table 3.3 further support the party disunity hypothesis, according to which the more a party exposes its differences on television at the convention, the less its chances will be for uniting and attracting Independent voters. The networks will devote additional coverage if there is a showdown at the convention, and viewers will be more likely to tune in to

Table 3.3 Convention television exposure, 1956–1988

	Democratic convention			Republican convention		
Year	Ratings	× Hours	= Exposure	Ratings	× Hours	= Exposure
1956	24.3	104	2527	29.4	65	1911
1960	29.3	79	2315	12.3[a]	73	898
1964	27.9	69	1925	20.4	103	2101
1968	28.8	81	2333	26.6	71	1889
1972	18.3[b]	92	1684	29.6	45	1332
1976	22.5	69	1553	25.2	73	1840
1980	24.8	56	1389	20.5	57	1169
1984	23.2	33	766	19.1	30	573
1988	20.6	31	639	18.7	35	655

Source: Byron E. Shafer, *Bifurcated Politics* (Cambridge, Mass.: Harvard University Press, 1988), p. 274; updated by the author for 1988.

a. The first session was held in the afternoon, thereby decreasing the ratings.

b. Includes ratings for the last session, which went until 4:00 A.M. (Eastern Daylight Time).

watch the fireworks. Yet what is good for drawing television attention to the convention is clearly bad for the party's chances in November. The 1960 election apparently marked the end of the era in which parties could survive nomination battles with relatively little effect. As Table 3.3 demonstrates, from 1964 to 1984 the party which received the most television convention exposure (as defined by ratings multiplied by hours) consistently lost.

In 1988 this pattern was broken because both dull conventions received little attention. The combined television ratings in 1988 were the lowest ever, with the highest rating any network garnered being an 8.7 for NBC on the night of Jackson's impassioned speech to the Democratic convention. By comparison, the following week CBS obtained a rating of 15.1 for its coverage of the Miss Teen USA Pageant.

The fact that both parties managed virtually to eradicate any conflict from their conventions in 1988 shows how each has learned its lesson from past defeats. It is a sad commentary on the future of nominating conventions to note that it has become conventional wisdom that a carefully scripted convention is the soundest electoral strategy. Thus, to use Walter Bagehot's terms, the national nominating convention has moved from being an efficient institution to a dignified one. The convention is no longer where the nomination is made any more than the British monarchy is where governing decisions are made in Britain; each plays a role only in legitimating choices made by more modern political institutions.

Although this sort of dignified status might be fitting for the British monarchy, it does not suit the American party convention very well. The convention is the best chance the parties have every four years to show the American public what they stand for and to demonstrate their role in the governmental process. Eliminating conflict and decision making from the conventions has had the effect of making the public more likely to neglect the parties and view them with indifference. With party organizations less institutionally relevant, they are less salient in the public mind, and therefore the party symbol no longer serves the unifying function it once did.

In fact the only event still likely to occur at future conventions is the choice of a running mate. The nominee's effort (if necessary) to assuage the dominant opposition faction via the selection of a vice president is the fourth and final stage at which the nomination process can lead to a divided party. The strongest possible statement of reconciliation is for the new nominee to select the runner-up for the nomination as the vice presidential candidate (as Reagan did in 1980). Alternatively, selecting someone who represents the ideological point of view of the runner-up (as Ford did in choosing Dole in 1976) will also help to mollify any division within the party. In contrast, as Polsby and Aaron Wildavsky write, "A refusal to heal the wounds and placate dissidents is nothing less than a declaration of internal war. It can only lead to increased conflict within the party."[17] Barry Goldwater's choice of William Miller in 1964 is one such example.

Even a widely popular choice is sometimes insufficient to heal the wounds of the primary season. The choice of Geraldine Ferraro, for instance, won much praise at the convention, but it did little to help draw Hart supporters back into the fold. Many Hart supporters apparently saw Ferraro's selection as just another example of Mondale's pandering to special interest groups.

And in 1988 the search for a Democratic vice presidential candidate clearly illustrated how this stage can prove to be a political minefield for a new nominee. The second place Democratic finisher, Jesse Jackson, not only said he would take the position but also insisted he had earned "serious consideration." When he was passed over for a southern conservative, the major story of the convention became whether the rift between Dukakis and Jackson could be healed. Dukakis aide John Corrigan expressed his camp's frustration with Jackson stealing the show when he told the Harvard campaign managers conference, "Our 15 minutes of being famous was being consumed by somebody else. And that inevitably did its damage."[18]

In sum, by adding together the number of indicators marked in Table 3.4, a rough index of "nomination fighting"

Table 3.4   Index of nomination fighting

Candidate	Early primary contests	Late primary contests	Convention battle	VP does not heal wounds	Total
Barry Goldwater (1964)	X	X	X	X	4
Lyndon Johnson (1964)					0
Richard Nixon (1968)			X	X	2
Hubert Humphrey (1968)	X	X	X	X	4
Richard Nixon (1972)					0
George McGovern (1972)	X	X	X	X	4
Gerald Ford (1976)	X	X	X		3
Jimmy Carter (1976)	X	X			2
Ronald Reagan (1980)	X				1
Jimmy Carter (1980)	X	X	X		3
Ronald Reagan (1984)					0
Walter Mondale (1984)	X	X		X	3
George Bush (1988)	X				1
Michael Dukakis (1988)	X	X		X	3

can be constructed ranging from zero to four. The greater the index figure, the more likely that the nominee's party identifiers have a divided opinion about him. Of course, some candidates are inherently more divisive than others because of their background or stands on various issues. To attempt to control for this factor, attitudes toward the candidate by members of the opposing party can be used as a baseline for comparison.

Ideally, a nominee would like to have his own party united about his candidacy while the opposition is divided toward him. In such a case, he can count on votes from most of his own party identifiers and a good number of Independents and members of the opposition party as well. Figure 3.1 displays how close each candidate in the 1964–1984 period came to this ideal situation. Positive entries mean that the candidate's own partisans were more unified in their evaluation of him than were the opposition party's identifiers. The unit of measurement is the standard deviation on the count of likes minus dislikes concerning him.

As can readily be seen, the greater the battle for the nomination, the more a nominee's party ends up divided about him in comparison to the opposition. The relationship is as close to being perfect as one is ever bound to find in social science. The only case which is somewhat out of line is that of Gerald Ford in 1976. Yet, as with all the other years, the pattern of standard deviations is 1976 is nevertheless quite consistent with the actual election results. Because Ford and Carter had virtually identical levels of party unity, one could have predicted a close race with the majority candidate winning by a narrow margin.

To play devil's advocate briefly, one might argue that both variables displayed in Figure 3.1 are little more than surrogate measures of candidate popularity. It might be that popular candidates are simply not strongly opposed for their par-

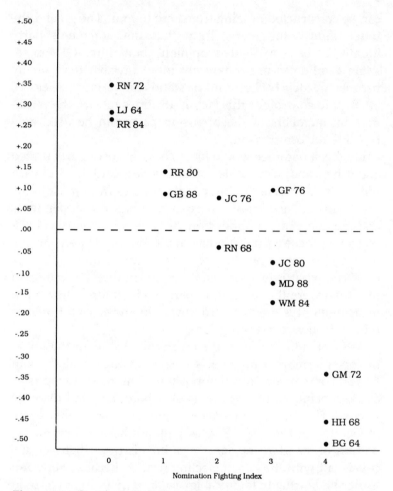

Figure 3.1   Standard deviation patterns of candidate ratings by index of nomination fighting. *Note:* Positive entries mean that the candidate's own partisans were more unified in their evaluation of him than were the opposition party's identifiers, as measured by the standard deviations.   *Source:* 1964–1988 SRC/CPS National Election Studies.

ty's leadership. Similarly, a candidate with many electoral assets should find it easier to maintain party unity.

I would argue that the causality between candidate popularity and party unity runs in both directions, however. A candidate with clear vulnerabilities will naturally encounter greater opposition for the nomination. In turn, the level of internal opposition plays a key role in determining the degree to which vulnerabilities are exacerbated. For instance, Edward Kennedy's decision to run in 1980 stemmed in large part from Carter's unpopularity, and his challenge further weakened Carter's chances of reelection. Yet Kennedy could well have chosen to end his campaign in April rather than fighting on to the convention in spite of hopeless odds. Thus, the key to the argument is that candidate decisions such as Kennedy's make an independent impact on party unity, which in turn greatly affects a nominee's chance for victory in November.

Humphrey in 1968 and Reagan in 1980 had nearly identical percentages of positive comments on the likes/dislikes questions, as shown in the next chapter. But the Democrats' primary and convention battles in 1968 were so divisive that Humphrey was able to hold onto only 68 percent of the Democratic vote in the general election—in spite of his respectable level of overall popularity. An even more striking example of the importance of party unity can be found in the data from 1984. In this case, the percentage of positive comments regarding Reagan was surprisingly similar to that for Mondale—51 versus 48 percent (see Figure 4.1). Yet the distribution of partisan opinion was more favorable for Reagan and is therefore crucial to understanding how he won a landslide victory.

Mondale probably lost what little chance he had to defeat Reagan in 1984 in the New Hampshire primary (of February 28), where his plans for quickly locking up the nomination were derailed by Gary Hart. During January and February of 1984, Democrats were somewhat more unified than Republicans in their evaluations of Mondale. As Table 3.5 shows, this difference all but evaporated in March as the battle with Hart got under way. The timing of this change in the distribution of attitudes is no mere coincidence. Had Mondale been as successful as Reagan in unifying his party during the nomination campaign year, he might have been able to give him a close race—the economic boom not withstanding. By sweeping the primaries and then adding Hart to the ticket, his chances in November would surely have been improved.

Table 3.5   Standard deviations of candidate feeling thermometer ratings (0–100 degrees) by party, 1984

Month	Mondale			Reagan		
	Republicans	Democrats	Difference	Democrats	Republicans	Difference
January	22.4	19.5	+2.9	28.0	21.8	+6.2
February	22.0	19.2	+2.8	28.8	17.2	+11.6
March	20.1	19.6	+0.5	26.0	18.2	+7.8
April	22.5	22.4	+0.1	30.1	18.7	+11.4
May	21.1	23.3	−2.2	28.6	20.6	+8.0
June	22.3	21.9	+0.4	28.7	22.3	+6.4
July	22.2	21.8	+0.4	30.1	18.7	+11.4
August	22.8	22.8	0.0	29.6	18.5	+11.1
September	23.4	25.9	−2.5	30.8	17.3	+13.5
October	20.9	23.9	−3.0	29.2	15.0	+14.2
November	22.7	24.2	−1.5	29.6	19.0	+10.6

Source: CPS Rolling Cross-Section Survey.

The Republican Advantage in the Age of Party Disunity

In the recent era of party disunity, the ideal path to victory has been a series of unbroken early primary wins, concessions from all the major contenders before the convention, and a harmonious convention that awards the second slot on the ticket to the leading opposition faction. Reagan's path to the nomination in 1980 and Bush's in 1988 followed this course. It is a course that puts the nominee in a good position to gain close to unanimous support from his own party and to attract a substantial proportion of Independents and identifiers with the opposition party.

While the electorate's focus has clearly been on the candidate not the party, it has been the harmony of the party which has been the key to candidate success since 1964. Since the Goldwater wing took over the party, the Republicans have been more ideologically cohesive and thus have acquired a natural advantage over the Democrats in this respect. Their nomination rules offer little incentive for primary losers to continue their campaigns, as delegates are frequently awarded in winner-take-all fashion. In contrast, the strict adherence to proportional representation in most Democratic primaries fosters "Timex" candidates—that is, candidates who "take a licking and keep on ticking." The longer losing campaigns for the nomination go on, the more likely they are to splinter the party.

A party which is divided in the spring and early summer— as the Democrats were throughout the 1980s—can no longer be easily reunited in the fall. As a result, a presidential candidate today does not have to be very popular to achieve a landslide victory; he need only keep his party relatively united while the opposition divides itself.

FOUR

Presidential Popularity in Decline

It is fascinating to note that in an electoral era centered on candidates the candidates themselves have become less and less popular. With the decline of partisanship in recent years, the influence of candidate evaluations has become less mediated and more direct. No longer are voters likely to unequivocably support a candidate just because he is the nominee of their party—particularly given the internal party criticism nominees now face during the primary season. This loss of automatic support has caused candidates for the presidency to be viewed in a far less positive light by the electorate. It seems that the more people come to know about the candidates, the less they like them. Familiarity has thus bred contempt.

Reagan's and Bush's relative lack of popularity compared to their predecessors can be seen as part of a long-term decline in the positivity of presidential candidate evaluations. The decline in presidential popularity is one of the most well documented trends in recent American politics.[1] Because of the regularity with which data are available from commercial polls it has been possible for academics to investigate theories of cycles of presidential popularity,[2] as well as the effects of specific factors such as international crises and economic fluctuations.[3] The academic community thereby greatly profits from the wealth of data points provided by Gallup's simple approval/disapproval item. Nevertheless, these data are of limited value because of the vagueness of the question and the general inability to determine the meaning of the responses from either more specific survey questions or open-ended queries. Rather than relying solely on the approval/disapproval item to assess popularity, this chapter employs open-ended data from the 1952–1988 National Election Studies (NES) to place the popularity of the presidential candidates of the 1980s in historical perspective.

The Reagan Popularity Myth

Probably no single aspect of the elections of the 1980s is more widely accepted than the immense personal popularity of Ronald Reagan. In 1980 Reagan became the first candidate to defeat an elected sitting incumbent since 1932, besting President Carter by 10 percent in the popular vote and carrying forty-four states. Four years later he crushed Democratic nominee Walter Mondale by 18 percentage points and came within a few thousand votes in Minnesota of becoming the first candidate ever to win all fifty states. And in 1988 Bush rode on the coattails of Reagan's 60-percent approval rating to carry forty states.

To many observers these electoral landslides are *prima facie* evidence of Reagan's great popularity with the public, and most would readily agree that his personality traits and general likeability had much to do with it. Even as severe a critic of the Reagan administration as historian Robert Dallek concedes that "few Americans in this century have enjoyed greater popularity than Ronald Reagan. Humor, charm, good looks, an intuitive feel for national concerns, and an extraordinary ability to speak persuasively to millions of people partly explain Reagan's popularity as governor of California and president."[4] As former speaker Tip O'Neill once said, "Ronald Reagan is the best-liked figure in American public life in memory." Similarly, Reagan's 1984 opponent, Walter Mondale, frankly remarked that he liked President Reagan personally, and in his press conference the day after the election began his list of reasons for his defeat with the statement that he was "running against a popular incumbent who was well liked personally" and who had a much better television presence than he did.

From the early days of his administration, Reagan's smoothness in television appearances and his seeming success in appealing to the public for support led the press to dub him the "Great Communicator." This reflected a popular belief that Reagan's televised speeches on behalf of his budget and tax proposals mobilized the needed public support to pressure Congress to enact them. But as Elliot King and Michael Schudson have persuasively argued, Reagan earned this reputation in the press "not because of special skills in communicating directly to the American people but because of significant skill in communicating with key elites, including the media itself."[5] They cite four factors as being crucial to the establishment of the Great Communicator image:

(1) the skill of Reagan and his staff in personally communicating with the press and other elites

(2) a changed balance of power in Washington after the 1980 election

(3) Reagan's ability to mobilize his core right wing constituency

(4) the exaggerated importance that the media and Washington insiders attribute to the role of television in shaping public opinion[6]

In particular, television had proven to be the Achilles heel for several recent presidents, but for Reagan it seemed to be a distinct asset. When he entered office the accepted scholarly wisdom was that television exposure had made the presidency a more powerful institution. At the same time presidents had been rapidly losing popularity because of television reporters' eagerness to pounce on every misstep and failure. [7] As George Bush said only partly in jest at the 1988 Al Smith dinner, he had learned that "a slip of the tongue is a gaffe, and a gaffe is a two-day story, and a two-day story is a trend." For Ronald Reagan, however, television was a modern version of Teddy Roosevelt's bully pulpit rather than the bearer of bad news and declining popularity that it had been for many of his predecessors.

This is not to say that the press did not amply criticize Reagan during his first term or that presidential failures were absent. Reagan's first term was far from smooth sailing, as witnessed by the rise in unemployment to a post–World War II high, a failed military operation in Lebanon, controversies involving cabinet members and presidential advisers, and numerous misstatements by the president himself. The second term got off to a shaky start with the ill-advised visit to the Nazi cemetery in Bitburg, West Germany, and then encountered its most serious problem with the Iran-Contra scandal. Whereas many of these storms would have sunk other presidents, Reagan emerged time and again without any seemingly permanent damage to his popularity. This continuing pattern led Representative Pat Schroeder to label the Reagan administration the "Teflon-coated presidency"— because nothing bad seemed to stick to it.

The most commonly cited explanation for this phenomenon was Reagan's personal charm, which enabled him to shrug off failures with a smile and an optimistic sense that everything would be all right in the end. As the noted scholar of presidential character James David Barber has written,

> Reagan's was not the charm of the simpering sycophant, but
> the man-to-man Jimmy Stewart charm, the charm of apparent
> sincerity, the charm of the impending smile . . . Reagan in
> person was as hard to dislike as a laughing baby, as many a
> hardbitten reporter had discovered. As president, Reagan
> added to that personal appeal the mighty effect of the official
> aura, which has reduced so many critics and skeptics to wor-
> shipful helplessness.[8]

Although Reagan was seen by many as an enormously
popular president who enjoyed widespread affection and ad-
miration from the public, the evidence from the 1980, 1984,
and 1988 NES data does *not* support such an interpretation at
all. This is not to say that the NES questions reveal patterns
either at variance with or completely invisible to the commercial pollsters. In fact, these surveys show virtually the same
approval rating for Reagan as commercial polls taken at the
same time. The difference is that the latter typically stop with
the approval measure, reporting this summary measure as if
it were all that mattered. When commercial polls included
additional specific approval questions, they too found that
hidden behind Reagan's high overall rating were numerous
negative assessments. For example, in August of 1986—one
of the high points of the Reagan presidency—a Harris poll
found that 60 percent of the public approved of Reagan's
handling of the presidency despite the fact that he had negative ratings of: 68 percent on his handling of the deficit; 64
percent on his dealings with South Africa; 60 percent on the
unemployment rate; 59 percent on his handling of Central
American involvement; 58 percent on his handling of affirmative action; and 54 percent on his call for a constitutional
amendment banning abortion. The open-ended questions in
the NES study allow us to assess whether such doubts are
indeed relevant to voters when they evaluate the candidates.

In addition, the closed-ended data concerning particular candidate traits enable us to investigate personal popularity in greater detail than with NES surveys prior to 1980.

The Decline of Candidate Popularity as Evidenced by Open-Ended Responses

The basic advantages and disadvantages of the open-ended questions about the candidates have already been touched upon in Chapter 1. For the purposes of this chapter, though, the specific advantages of open-ended questions over the simple Gallup approval/disapproval measure should be noted. Most obvious is that one can pinpoint the factors behind people's evaluations. Respondents can identify whatever is important to them about the candidates, regardless of whether or not the designers of the survey might think of such considerations. This is of special value for time series purposes since it is difficult to write closed-ended questions that are relevant from one decade to another. With these open-ended questions one can compare the strengths and weaknesses of candidates in different elections in a manner uncontaminated by the perspectives of the authors of the questions or changes in research methodology.

Another major advantage is that by probing for both likes and dislikes it is possible to determine whether those who approve of a candidate nevertheless have reservations, or whether those who disapprove have some positive feelings toward the candidate. For example, although Reagan had a very high approval rating of 63 percent in the 1984 sample, the open-ended data reveal that nearly half (45 percent) of those who approved of his handling of the presidency had some reason why they might be inclined to vote against him—a figure greater than for any other incumbent for whom data are available.

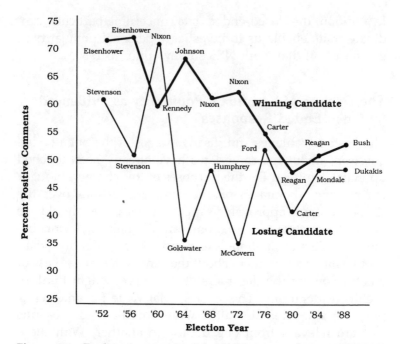

Figure 4.1 Decline in presidential candidate popularity, 1952–1988 (voters only).   *Source:* SRC/CPS National Election Studies.

The easiest way to derive a general assessment of candidate popularity from these data is to calculate the proportion of comments which were positive in each case. Figure 4.1 presents this percentage for all presidential candidates from 1952 to 1988 among the voting participants in each year. From this figure it can be readily seen that neither Reagan nor Bush was as popular overall as their recent predecessors. Averaging the three elections of the 1980s, one finds that only 50.2 percent of voters' comments about Reagan or Bush were positive.

In contrast, from 1952 to 1964 responses concerning the most popular candidate were regularly about 70 percent positive. This was true not only for war-hero Eisenhower, but for Johnson as well, and strangely enough, for Nixon in 1960. The fact that Nixon was actually viewed more favorably than Kennedy in 1960 is a telling indicator of the greater importance of candidate evaluations in recent years. It is inconceivable in the candidate-centered age that a major party nominee could lose in spite of being significantly more popular with the voters.

With the decline of candidate popularity, however, it was possible for Reagan to win in 1980 even though voters had more to say about why they wouldn't vote for him than why they would. Whereas party loyalty saved the day for Kennedy, it was the extreme dissatisfaction with Carter in 1980 that allowed Reagan to win the presidency with an incredibly weak public image. Of all the candidates prior to 1980, only Barry Goldwater in 1964 and George McGovern in 1972—each the victim of a landslide—received lower ratings than Reagan. The difference of course is that Reagan's 1980 opponent, President Carter, was seen even less favorably by a substantial margin.

By 1984 Reagan's net popularity had at least barely edged up into the positive range at 51 percent, but compared to reelected presidents before him, he ranked last. The percentage of positive comments for other reelected presidents was 71 for Eisenhower, 68 for Johnson, and 62 for Nixon. Considering that Mondale's popularity was about average for losing candidates while Reagan's popularity was low for a winner, the landslide margin of the 1984 election seems quite puzzling.

To understand this perplexing finding, it is necessary to examine voters' ratings of the candidates according to whom they voted for. Figure 4.2 charts the popularity of winning candidates from 1952 to 1984 among their voting supporters and opponents. We can see that Reagan's low 1984 popular-

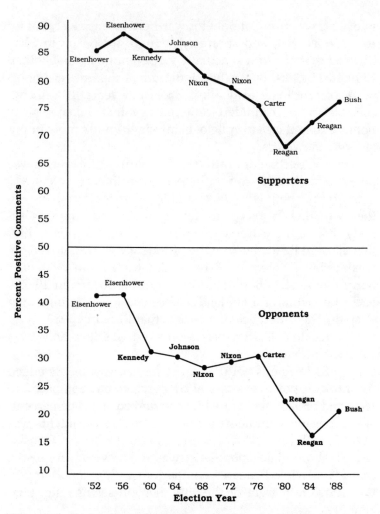

Figure 4.2 Evaluations of winning candidates by voting supporters and opponents. *Source:* SRC/CPS National Election Studies.

ity stemmed largely from the unprecedented intense dislike with which he was met by voters who opposed him. Whereas Reagan's supporters liked him somewhat better in 1984 than in 1980, his opponents liked him even less in the second election than in the first. From 1960 to 1976 comments about the winning candidate from those who supported the loser were typically about 30 percent positive, Eisenhower's great personal appeal enabled him to do substantially better than this in the 1950s, with over 40 percent of opponents' comments being positive. But in 1984 Reagan's image among his opponents clearly went from bad to worse. Only 16 percent of the comments about Reagan by Mondale voters were positive—roughly half the standard set by his presidential predecessors. Furthermore, this phenomenon continued in 1988 without Reagan on the ballot. The proportion of positive comments about Bush from opposition voters was just 21 percent—the lowest figure ever for a newly elected president.

Because candidates attract so much attention in politics today, they engender stronger feelings than ever before. Those who do not support a candidate increasingly feel that there is little good about him and are more aware of his bad points. Also damaging to candidate popularity is that with the decline of party loyalty the notion of "my candidate, right or wrong" has faded considerably. Thus, a candidate's supporters are more likely to express doubts about him than in the past.

To illustrate these points, positive and negative voting reasons regarding winning candidates can be examined for the presence of four informative patterns that percentages alone may obscure. For supporters, it is important to ascertain how many were strongly for the candidate as well as how many had doubts about their choice. The former will be defined by the percentage with greater than two positive comments

Table 4.1 Evaluations of newly elected presidential candidates

	1952 Eisenhower	1960 Kennedy	1968 Nixon	1976 Carter	1980 Reagan	1988 Bush
Percentage of supporters with > 2 positive comments	52.8	43.7	59.3	36.5	30.0	39.2
Percentage of supporters with a negative comment	32.6	29.6	39.6	44.1	53.4	41.5
Percentage of opponents with > 2 negative comments	13.7	21.8	26.0	26.7	31.2	35.2
Percentage of opponents with a positive comment	50.6	41.0	31.4	42.3	30.2	28.2

Source: SRC/CPS National Election Studies.
Note: For 1968 and 1980 Wallace and Anderson voters are classified as opponents of the presidential winner.

whereas the latter can be determined by the percentage with any reason for voting against the candidate. For nonsupporters, we need to know just the opposite—how many were strongly against (that is, had more than two negative comments) as well as how many could think of a reason for voting for the winner, even though they did not. Finally, in order to control for the effects of incumbency, these data are presented in two separate tables. Table 4.1 displays the data for candidates elected to the presidency for the first time, and Table 4.2 contains the figures for reelected incumbents.

Data in the first table support the conclusion that Reagan did not come to office in 1980 with widespread enthusiasm among those who voted for him. Fewer of Reagan's 1980 voters could be classified as strong supporters than those of

Table 4.2 Evaluations of reelected presidential incumbents

	1956 Eisenhower	1964 Johnson	1972 Nixon	1984 Reagan
Percent of supporters with > 2 positive comments	56.8	44.2	40.1	51.7
Percentage of supporters with a negative comment	29.4	29.3	31.6	48.3
Percentage of opponents with > 2 negative comments	21.3	28.3	31.4	54.1
Percentage of opponents with a positive comment	59.7	39.3	39.9	27.1

Source: SRC/CPS National Election Studies.

any previous winning candidate since 1952. Only 30 percent fit this category compared to an average of 48 percent for previous nonincumbent winners. In addition, Reagan set an all-time high in 1980 for the percentage of supporters with some stated reservation about their choice (53 percent). Thus the low mean rating Reagan received from his own voters at the time of his first election (see Figure 4.2) can be explained by the lack of enthusiasm as well as by the significant doubts his supporters had about him.

On the other side of the political fence, Reagan did unusually poorly with his opponents as well. Those who voted for a losing candidate in 1980 were more likely to express strong negative feelings and less likely than ever before to say anything positive about a newly elected presidential candidate. For the first time, a winning candidate had more opponents in the latter category than in the former, albeit by a slight margin.

By 1984, however, this margin was no longer slight. In fact it was two to one—with 54 percent of Mondale voters having more than two reasons for voting against Reagan compared to only 27 percent who expressed any positive comment about him. In contrast, the comparable figures for Eisenhower in 1956 were virtually the reverse—21 and 60 percent, respectively. Thus, while Eisenhower was extraodinarily successful in evoking positive comments from those who did not favor continuing with his administration, Reagan was exceptional in engendering dislike among voters who wanted to hold him to just one term. Even Ford and Carter, who were denied reelection, did not face as many opposing voters with strong negative feelings about them.

Reagan and Eisenhower are similar only in their ability to elicit numerous positive feelings from their supporters. These two were the only incumbent presidents for whom more than 50 percent of their voters qualify as strong supporters. Yet, despite this similarity on the positive side, Reagan supporters were nearly 20 percentage points more likely than Eisenhower's to express negative comments. In other words, Reagan's voters were more favorable toward him in 1984 than in 1980, but their unprecedented degree of doubts remained.

One might say that Reagan polarized his supporters as well as his opponents. Certainly polarization is the major message to emerge from the 1984 data on Reagan, Furthermore, there is ample evidence from Gallup data gathered during the course of Reagan's first term that polarization was not simply a short-term campaign artifact. From Eisenhower to Carter the average difference in monthly presidential approval scores between Democrats and Republicans was 35 percentage points. Under Reagan, the gap increased to 54 percentage points, with an average of 83 percent of Republicans approving compared to only 29 percent for Democrats. As George Edwards notes, the greater degree of polarization with regard to Reagan was due to the especially low ratings of him by Democrats.[9] This finding matches nicely with the data displayed in Figure 4.2, showing that the polarization Reagan induced during the 1984 campaign was mostly the result of the unprecedented degree of dislike among his opponents.

This pattern continued throughout Reagan's second term,[10] and in 1988 with regard to the candidacy of George Bush. Returning to Table 4.1, we see that Bush came into office with the lowest percentage of opponents making a positive comment about him and the highest percentage having more than two negative comments. Compared to Reagan in 1980, though, Bush did better among his own voters. But as with Carter and Reagan before him, among Bush's supporters more had something negative to say about him than expressed strong positive support. In contrast, Eisenhower, Kennedy, and Nixon all were initially elected to office with more strong supporters than doubters.

The open-ended data on voters' evaluation of Bush in 1988 confirms two important trends in evaluations of winning presidential candidates: the overall decline in popularity and the polarization of opinion. Although Bush received a slightly higher percentage of positive comments from the voters than Reagan, his popularity ranked below all the other winning candidates since 1952. The downslide in presidential candidate popularity thus seems to have stabilized at a new, much lower, level. Apparently, the more people know about a political figure, the more likely they are to find something that displeases them.

Indeed, as one goes up the hierarchy of political visibility one finds more negative evaluations from the voters. Whereas just 51 percent of the comments about Bush and Dukakis were positive in 1988, open-ended questions about Senate candidates yielded positive comments 65 percent of the time, and House candidates were the most popular of all at 74 percent.[11] Candidates may be more concerned with publicity than ever before, but visibility apparently comes with significant risks to a politician's image—especially with the weakening of bedrock partisan support.

As one moves from House to Senate to presidential candidates, greater polarization of opinion can also be found. The 1988 data on Bush confirm that as presidential candidates have become more salient, opinions about them have become more polarized. Returning to Figure 4.2, we can see that the gap between supporters and opponents of the winning candidate was the highest ever in 1984 and the second highest ever in 1988. Another way of measuring polarization is the feeling thermometer, a standardized zero-to-one-hundred scale which dates back to 1968. The evidence from these data are quite consistent with the open-ended measures. When asked to rate Reagan in 1984, the mean difference of 45 points between his supporters and opponents was 10 points greater than for any other winning candidate before him, and the mean difference of 39 points in 1988 ratings of Bush is the second highest in the time series.

It should be noted that this increase in candidate polarization contrasts sharply with the trend in open-ended responses about the parties, which have rapidly moved away from polarized opinions toward neutrality. In part, the greater polarization in candidate evaluations during the 1980s is a natural replacement for the political polarization formerly centered on the parties.[12]

Personal Attributes of the Candidates

As the candidates themselves have received more attention during the presidential campaign, their character and ability have been scrutinized more carefully. Because so much power is vested in one person alone, the personal attributes of the candidates are clearly relevant factors to be discussed in the campaign. Even before presidential actions had immediate world-wide consequences, personal behavior and characteristics were often an important consideration. Scurrilous attacks on candidates' personal lives were commonplace in the nineteenth century. Yet most people took these charges for what they were—partisan gesturing through the partisan press. The dignity of those seeking the office remained high, and candidates did not engage in personal attacks themselves. It is the transition to debating through television commercials that has involved the candidates far more directly in disparaging each other's reputation. This has given such charges greater credibility, as has the fact they are now reported through a largely nonpartisan press.

Thus there is good reason to expect that the focus on personal attributes has been a major component of the decline in candidate popularity. If so, this would run against the popular notion that highly favorable views of Reagan's personality were an important asset in his electoral victories. To test whether Reagan's much discussed charm and perceived leadership qualities were seen as positively as many believe, it is necessary to examine the open-ended questions in historical context for the presence of such evaluations.

Comments about a candidate's personal attributes can be divided into five general categories—integrity, reliability, competence, charisma, and the candidate's appearance/demographic characteristics.[13] The first, integrity, deals with the candidate as trustworthy or untrustworthy and incorporates comments concerning honesty, sincerity, and any reference to corruption in government. The second, reliability, is similar to the first with some important distinctions: reliability refers to a candidate being dependable, strong, decisive, aggressive, stable, or the converse of these. That these two dimensions are separate is most evident in the 1964 evaluations of Goldwater, in which he received the highest rating on integrity of any candidate except Eisenhower and the lowest reliability rating of any candidate in the thirty-six-year series. Reliability can be seen as a bridge between the integrity and competence attributes. Perhaps the best definition of it would be: trust in the sense of "capability" rather than in the sense of "honesty." Competence itself refers to the candidate's past political experience, ability as a statesman, comprehension of political issues, realism, and intelligence. In contrast, charisma involves less tangible considerations, such as a candidate's leadership abilities, dignity, humbleness, patriotism, and ability to get along and communicate with people. The last attribute has to do with various personal aspects of the candidate, including appearance, age, religion, wealth, former occupation, family, and so on.

Table 4.3 summarizes how each candidate from 1952 to 1988 was perceived by the public on these five personality dimensions. The trend over time clearly demonstrates a decline in positive evaluations, particularly with regard to candidate competence. Rather than reversing this trend, Reagan clearly played a large part in its continuation. In fact, a comparison of Reagan's 1980 image on these five aspects to that of previous newly elected presidents, and of his 1984 image to that of other incumbents, reveal notable weaknesses and little sign of the famous Reagan personal magic.

Among all the candidates in the time series only Barry Goldwater and George McGovern did worse than Ronald Reagan in 1980 on all five combined. The primary reason for this was Reagan's extremely low score on the "personal" comments in 1980. Since the days of Eisenhower's military background and Kennedy's Catholicism, remarks fitting into this miscellaneous category have not figured prominently in respondent's answers. When Reagan was first nominated for president, however, his age and former occupation as an

Table 4.3 Personality evaluations of presidential candidates (and Reagan in 1988)

	Competence	Integrity	Reliability	Charisma	Personal
Incumbent Presidents					
Eisenhower (1956)	+43	+25	0	+17	+10
Johnson (1964)	+50	−13	+3	+8	+1
Nixon (1972)	+33	−8	+6	+1	+1
Ford (1976)	+25	+2	−7	−1	+1
Carter (1980)	+13	+2	−7	−1	+1
Reagan (1984)	+12	+2	+8	+6	−7
Reagan (1988)	−7	−3	0	+9	+1
Non-incumbent winners					
Eisenhower (1952)	+15	+22	+3	+18	+14
Kennedy (1960)	+23	+7	+7	+1	−15
Nixon (1968)	+29	−2	−8	−3	+4
Carter (1976)	−1	0	−9	0	+8
Reagan (1980)	+3	−1	−3	0	−18
Bush (1988)	+28	−2	0	−2	+1
Non-incumbent losers					
Stevenson (1952)	+33	+6	+1	+4	+1
Stevenson (1956)	+16	0	−1	−4	−8
Nixon (1960)	+47	+2	+4	+5	+11
Goldwater (1964)	0	+11	−25	−1	0
Humphrey (1968)	+20	+4	−8	−4	−3
McGovern (1972)	−11	−1	−16	−1	−1
Mondale (1984)	0	0	−5	−3	0
Dukakis (1988)	−5	0	+1	−2	0

Source: SRC/CPS National Election Studies.

Note: Means have been calculated by adding the number of positive responses and subtracting the number of negative responses for each respondent. The result is then multiplied by 100 to remove the decimal point.

actor drew numerous negative responses. Over 13 percent of those interviewed spontaneously mentioned Reagan's age as a reason why they might vote against him, making this by far the most common response to the question. And 5 percent said they would be inclined to vote against Reagan because he was an actor—also a substantial percentage for an open-ended response. Despite the greater prevalence of the age issue, it was not strongly related to the vote choice in 1980. Fifty percent of the voters who mentioned it apparently wrote it off as a minor reservation and cast their ballots for Reagan anyway, compared to only 24 percent of those who voiced a negative opinion about having a former actor as president. The probable explanation for this difference is that the latter factor was more deeply politicized than the former. Being an actor was seen by many as reflecting a lack of political experience and competence, whereas the age issue evoked concerns about whether Reagan would complete his term rather than whether he would do well in the job.

Examining comments specifically about Reagan's competence in 1980, one finds that he did slightly better than Carter in 1976, but the +3 score pales in comparison to the figures for Nixon, Kennedy, and Eisenhower when they were first elected. Like Carter, who had been governor of Georgia for only one term, Reagan's record in public service was seen as lacking by many voters. Similarly, Reagan and Carter did poorly on integrity when first elected, with the number of responses about their honesty roughly equaling the number saying they were dishonest. Reliability was even more of a problem for both, but here the negative responses differ. This was Carter's major personality weakness in 1976 as a result of the perception that he was indecisive and prone to flip-flopping on issues. Reagan's reliability problem, in contrast, was primarily due to statements regarding his perceived impulsiveness and carelessness in judgment. Finally, on charisma the positive comments about Reagan being inspiring and a man one can follow were equally balanced in 1980 by comments about him being a poor leader because he didn't understand the nation's problems. In sum, Reagan's image was unimpressive compared to previous non-incumbent winning candidates. Certainly one cannot say that Reagan attained office on the strengths of a winning personality, as one might say about Eisenhower.

It might be presumed that by 1984 all of this had changed owing to the largely favorable press coverage of Reagan as a person throughout his first term. Indeed, Reagan's image improved noticeably on all five personality attributes between 1980 and 1984. But compared to other incumbent presidents Reagan's personal popularity remained below average. Adding the five attributes together shows that Reagan did only one point better than Ford and substantially worse than Eisenhower, Johnson, and Nixon when they ran for reelection.

In particular, Reagan did worse than any other previous sitting president on competence, which has traditionally been a major source of the incumbency advantage. If nothing else, an incumbent can usually count on a large number of people remarking that he is experienced in the job. This was true for Reagan as well, but to a significantly reduced degree. In 1980, 10.0 percent of all interviewees said that Carter's experience in office made them inclined to vote for him, whereas only 2.5 percent made similar positive comments about Reagan in 1984. Furthermore, these were partly counterbalanced in 1984 by comments about Reagan's seeming lack of knowledge and by perceptions of him being managed by his staff. Fortunately for Reagan, many more people said that he had gotten things done than said so with reference to

Carter in 1980. Were it not for this factor, Reagan's 1984 competence rating would have been the worst for any incumbent by a large instead of a small margin.

On two dimensions the data do indicate some support for the vaunted Reagan personal strength—reliability and charisma. First, he received the highest score ever in 1984 on reliability. Of the five attributes, reliability has been the only one on which candidates have consistently drawn more negative than positive responses. Against this background, the positive comments regarding Reagan's decisiveness and stability are particularly notable. Similarly, over the last two decades only Lyndon Johnson received a score substantially above 0 on the charisma dimension, thereby making the 1984 comments about Reagan being an inspiring leader all the more impressive.

When people were asked in 1988 what they liked and disliked about what Reagan had done as president, charisma remained the personality dimension which drew the most favorable comments. Yet, as a result of the Iran-Contra affair, his ratings on competence, integrity, and reliability all fell noticeably. The scandal brought home more clearly than ever before that Reagan was not a hands-on executive and also weakened his claims to honesty and dependability. Thus although Reagan did not leave office because of an unpopular war, a scandal, or an election defeat—as did his last four predecessors—he nevertheless left with a tarnished personal image.

At the same time, Bush was elected to office with a relatively good personal image—at least on the most important attribute, competence. The favorable perceptions of Bush's competence can be traced to comments about his long experience in governmental office and foreign affairs. Indeed, his competence score of $+28$ was second only to Nixon's in 1968 for newly elected presidents. Still, the appropriate comparison for Bush is not so much Nixon in 1968 as Nixon in 1960. In both cases, the vice president ran on his experience as understudy to a successful two-term president. Although Nixon lost, his rating exceeded that of Bush on all five attributes—most notably on competence. Seen in this perspective, the 1988 data on Bush again indicate the much lower level of personal popularity in the candidate-centered age.

If even winning candidates of the 1980s are rated below losing candidates of three decades ago, then obviously the losers of the 1980s also suffer by comparison. Vice President Mondale's 1984 ratings thus fell well below the 1968 ratings of his mentor, Vice President Humphrey. Similarly, Governor Dukakis did not even approach the level of personal respect enjoyed by Governor Stevenson in 1952.

Closed-Ended Candidate Trait Ratings

This is not to say that the Republican candidates of the 1980s dominated the Democratic candidates across the board on personality. Many of the weaknesses of Reagan and Bush referred to above can be confirmed by comparing how they are assessed relative to their opponents on a series of closed-ended candidate trait ratings. These closed-ended questions, which were first introduced to the NES in 1980, provide an important complement to the open-ended data. One potential drawback in using the open-ended material is that different people employ different dimensions of evaluation. While this has the advantage of demonstrated saliency, those who are concerned enough about a given subject may be atypical of the population as a whole. Many respondents may not mention anything about a given trait, but when asked directly about it will clearly rate one candidate above the other.

As displayed in Table 4.4, the largest advantage for any

Table 4.4 Voters' comparison of candidates' personal traits

Trait	Reagan versus Carter, 1980	Reagan versus Mondale, 1984	Reagan versus Dukakis, 1988	Bush versus Dukakis, 1988
Strength				
Provides strong leadership	+31.4	+32.1	+17.4	−2.7
Inspiring	+16.2	+24.8	+20.4	−9.7
Weak	+39.9	—	—	—
Commands respect	—	+31.6	—	—
Capability				
Knowledgeable	−2.3	+1.4	−7.2	+7.6
Intelligent	—	+8.7	−16.8	−11.8
Hard-working	—	−22.5	—	—
Integrity				
Moral	−19.7	+11.5	+7.9	+8.0
Dishonest/honest	−5.2	—	−11.2	−8.6
Decent	—	+6.8	+8.6	+11.5
Power-hungry	−11.7	—	—	—
Sets a good example	—	+11.8	—	—

Source: CPS National Election Studies.

Note: Table entries are the percentage of voters rating the Republican more favorably minus the percentage rating the Democrat more favorably.

candidate in the 1980s was for Reagan on the candidate traits labeled "strength." Reagan was consistently rated much better than the Democratic nominee on the terms "provides strong leadership" and "inspiring" throughout the 1980s. He was also rated highly favorably on "commands respect" when this was asked in 1984 and was seen as far less "weak" than Carter in 1980. These traits correspond best to the charisma dimension on the open-ended questions, on which Reagan also did extremely well.

However, while voters were confident that Reagan would provide strength of character in the White House, they were not impressed with his mental ability to handle the presidency or his commitment to work hard at it. As Thomas Cronin has written, "One of the paradoxes of the Reagan presidency is that while Americans view Ronald Reagan as a strong leader, they also view him as a semidetached chief executive, an executive who lets several of his key advisers make most of the important decisions in the White House."[14] Reagan's poor ratings on the open-ended competence dimension are matched by the closed-ended comparisions on the traits labeled "capability." Again, the 1988 data show a noticeable drop, no doubt due to the revelations resulting from the Iran-Contra scandal.

In spite of the duplicity uncovered in this scandal, Reagan continued to do relatively well on two of three traits labeled "integrity" in Table 4.4. Only his reputation for honesty suffered in 1988. Yet it should be noted that integrity was never Reagan's strong suit. Indeed, he was somewhat at a disadvantage to Carter on this in 1980. If nothing else, Carter had successfully cultivated the image of an honest president who always tried to do what he thought was morally right. In 1984, against an opponent who drew less attention to these qualities, Reagan did better on integrity than he had in 1980.

Finally, comparing Bush and Dukakis in 1988 reinforces the interpretation of the open-ended data that Bush did not have strong personal appeal to the voters. Bush's long experience in government may have given him a quite respectable score on the open-ended competence measure, but he split the two capability items with Dukakis, rating more knowledgeable but less intelligent. Bush was rated worse on both strength items than Dukakis, who in turn was seen as much less inspiring or able to provide strong leadership than Reagan. And on integrity Bush had the same advantage enjoyed by Reagan in terms of decency and morality, but he also had the same disadvantage on honesty because of suspicions about his role in the diversion of money to the Contras.

Contrary to the notion that to be better known is a political asset, increased attention has actually led presidential candidates to become less popular over time. Despite the media hype about Reagan's charm, the survey data reveal a public which was not terribly taken with the man. It may be that he conveyed an image as a "nice guy" through the media, but if so very little of this was politicized—and therefore present in the candidate assessments reviewed here. Nor was the "Teflon-coated" presidency all that the popular press played it up to be, as there is certainly strong evidence of major negatives "sticking" to Reagan. The arrows shot at Reagan may have been cushioned with suction cups as opposed to having sharp points, but they did stick to his public image.

The survey results show Reagan to be the least popular candidate to win election to the presidency since the election studies began in 1952. In 1980, and especially in 1984, he was disliked with unprecedented intensity by those who opposed him and supported with an unusual degree of doubt by his backers. Furthermore, this polarization and relatively low level of popularity was continued in 1988 by the Bush candidacy. Although certain features of the data on Reagan are surely idiosyncratic to him (comments about him being an actor, being run by his staff, and so on), the general pattern reveals important dimensions of change in candidate evaluations since the 1950s.

At several points in this chapter, public evaluations of Reagan have been contrasted to those of Eisenhower. Both had high approval ratings throughout most of their time in office, yet Eisenhower enjoyed much stronger support from the electorate in response to open-ended questions. Unlike Reagan, Eisenhower was a relatively nonpartisan and un-ideological figure. He managed to win acclaim by saying that he would go to Korea, but never said what he would do there. And on the most controversial issue of the day—civil rights—he was able to skirt the issue. Had he been forced to deal with these issues head-on in the campaign, voters no doubt would have made more negative comments about him. Thus, the differences between evaluations of Reagan and Eisenhower have as much to do with the different time periods involved as with the individuals.

With this lower level of public support and the rise of ticket splitting, it is a wonder that presidents are ever able to exercise much influence with Congress. Certainly Reagan was able to and accomplished much of what he set out to do in 1981 by claiming a public mandate. Assessing the evidence for such a policy mandate is the aim of the next chapter.

FIVE

Was There a Mandate?

Unlike the question of Ronald Reagan's popularity, the degree to which he did or did not have a policy mandate was controversial from the outset. Issue voting has been one of the most important and widely researched subjects in American political science, and the extent to which issues affect electoral choices has been hotly debated for decades.[1] In the candidate-centered age, this debate is all the more important as a president's political capital has come to be based more on perceptions of his personal mandate than on the strength of his political party. Issues, like candidates, have become more central to determining the vote as political parties have declined. Yet there are two distinct types of issue mandates—policy and performance—and this chapter argues that in the case of the elections of the 1980s the former was largely absent.

Virtually any topic that is discussed in a political campaign involves reasonable disagreements between the candidates and can therefore be considered an issue. As Donald Stokes pointed out long ago, it is important to distinguish issues on which candidates agree about the basic goals from those on which they take distinct positions.[2] The former Stokes termed "valence issues," in that they link the candidates with some condition that is either positively or negatively valued by the electorate, such as peace and prosperity. What is critical in this case is not the means by which a problem is solved, but rather whether or not the goal is attained. In contrast, what Stokes termed "position issues" deal with alternative public policies. Stokes's distinction is critical for drawing appropriate substantive interpretations from election outcomes. In the former, a policy message is conveyed by the voters; in the latter, voters merely reward or punish based on performance considerations. I will refer to these two theories of voting behavior as policy voting and performance voting.

In both types, dissatisfaction with the current state of governmental affairs leads to voting for the challenger over the incumbent, as happened in 1980. However, the theory behind policy voting adds the postulate that dissatisfaction leads to changes in the electorate's policy preferences. Not satisfied with what the government is doing, many voters turn to new alternatives and to leaders who will implement these new policy objectives. E.E. Schattschneider has argued that elections act as an endorsement of a general policy orientation, although not necessarily as a guide for initiating specific policies.[3] According to this view, the 1980 electorate may not have been endorsing particular changes in federal spending and the 1984 and 1988 electorates ratifying them, but nevertheless all three electorates could be interpreted as conveying a desire for a more conservative government.

In contrast, under performance voting political change is induced by negative assessments of the job the incumbent is doing, as opposed to an endorsement of the policy alternatives proposed by the challenger. Similarly, elections in which the incumbent party is reelected can be seen as evidence of satisfaction with the state of the economy and foreign affairs. Elections in this theory are at best a control mechanism by which incumbents can be removed from office if the public is dissatisfied with the results. What matters is not the policies that they pursue but only the outputs they produce. The "mandate" is merely to reach a desired performance level.

Although policy and performance issues may be easily differentiated conceptually, the relationship between them is a complicated matter evoking much important scholarly debate. The question of whether policy opinions generate performance evaluations or vice versa is difficult to assess, even with panel data. For example, in 1980 did public opinion in favor of conservative public policies cause discontent with President Carter, or did the perception of his failures cause people to rationalize their vote against him by espousing more conservative attitudes?

Different assumptions regarding causality yield remarkably different results. J. Merrill Shanks and Warren E. Miller, for instance, specify policies as causally prior to performance considerations in their multistage model of voting behavior in 1980 and 1984. This assumption leads them to the conclusion that desires for a more conservative government were a very important factor in Reagan's election and reelection.[4] Yet, employing the same data, Charles Franklin argues that there is a "systematic" adjustment of issue preferences in response to political evaluations and outcomes,"[5] and thus casts doubt on the specification of the Shanks and Miller model.

Rather than making an assumption one way or the other on the question of causality, I will deal with policy and performance factors largely on a separate basis—testing the plausibility of each as explanatory variables for the Reagan victories. Because policy issues are most crucial to the mandate question, the remainder of this chapter will be devoted to their role in the elections of the 1980s. A detailed investigation of performance assessments as an alternative explanation will follow in Chapter 6.

A More Conservative Electorate?

The evidence that governmental policies shifted to the right as a result of Reagan's election is beyond doubt, but there is almost no evidence that a movement toward conservatism occurred among the voting public. Given the shift of power in the 1980 elections, there was good reason to suspect a comparable rightward tilt in public opinion. Thus the press rushed to cover the behind the scenes stories of the conservative movement, with figures such as Jerry Falwell, Terry Dolan, and Richard Viguerie attracting much attention. In 1981, for example, there were 106 articles about the conservative movement printed in magazines indexed in the *Readers' Guide to Periodical Literature* compared to 57 in 1980 and 22 in 1979.[6] Yet despite the proclamations from the pundits that the conservative movement was on the rise, the survey data showed much to the contrary.

Prior to Reagan's 1980 election it had been accepted political wisdom that candidates who were too far from the ideological center—either left or right—could not be elected president. In 1964 the first crucial test of this theory was made possible by the nomination of Barry Goldwater, who in his own words offered "a choice rather than an echo," and took stands far to the right of any Republican nominee since the New Deal. Goldwater's extreme positions were widely blamed for his landslide defeat. Similarly, in 1972 the case of George McGovern showed that the same fate was likely to be encountered by a candidate positioned too far to the left of center.

The theory and the experience therefore both predicted that an ideological extremist like Reagan could not be elected and reelected unless the electorate were to move in a conservative direction. Some academics, such as Samuel Popkin—a participant in the Carter polling operation—even went on the record as saying a conservative movement had occurred. As Popkin wrote in 1984, "We are looking at fundamental ideological change in America."[7] However, the survey evidence, as shown in Table 5.1, does little to confirm this. There were only slightly more self-identified conservatives in the 1980s than previously, and affect toward conservatives and liberals remained virtually unchanged.

Since the 1972 election, NES respondents have been asked to place themselves on a seven-point scale, with 1 representing "extremely liberal," 4 "moderate," and 7 "extremely conservative." Because very few people opt for the extremes, the end points have been collapsed in the table to make for a

Table 5.1 Trends in political ideology

Self-placement scale	1972	1976	1980	1984	1988
Strong conservative	16.0	19.7	23.1	20.8	23.6
Weak conservative	20.8	18.5	21.0	20.1	21.7
Moderate	37.4	37.7	30.6	33.4	31.3
Weak liberal	13.7	12.0	13.5	12.9	13.1
Strong liberal	12.1	12.1	11.8	12.7	10.3

Mean feeling thermometer ratings of:	1964	1968	1972	1976	1980	1984	1988
Conservatives	56.8	56.9	61.4	58.9	62.7	59.9	61.1
Liberals	53.4	51.1	53.8	52.3	51.7	55.9	51.7

Source: SRC/CPS National Election Studies.

simpler five-point scale. Among the 60 to 70 percent who have thought enough about the question of ideology to place themselves on the scale, the figures in Table 5.1 indicate that conservatives did increase from 36.8 to 45.3 percent between 1972 and 1988. Yet most of this change came from a decrease in the moderate category and not from any substantial decline in self-identified liberals. George Bush may have succeeded in berating Michael Dukakis as a liberal, but he was only taking advantage of a long-standing public preference for the conservative label, which increased marginally during the 1980s.

Another method of measuring ideological attitudes is through feeling thermometer ratings of "liberals" and "conservatives," which were first introduced into the election studies in 1964. It is interesting to note that even as Goldwater was being defeated by a wide margin in 1964, ratings of "conservatives" were nevertheless more positive than those of "liberals." As the only major democratic country without a major socialist party, the United States has had a tradition of favoring the conservative label, and the data from 1964 are an excellent indication of this. Given that 1964 is the least likely year for feelings toward conservatives to be high, one would have to expect that any change in affect since then would be in a rightward direction. This is indeed the case, with the mean rating of "conservatives" rising to 62.7 in 1980 from the 1964 low of 56.8. As was found on the self-placement scale, liberal attitudes were more constant over time, declining only 1.7 points over the same period. In 1984 the mean rating of "liberals" actually reached a new high, but by 1988 the figures were back to where they were in 1980. In sum, there is little support for the thesis of fundamental ideological change. The picture is of stability rather than change on liberal-conservative attitudes in the electorate.

A More Ideologically Polarized Electorate?

Although the distribution of liberals and conservatives has barely changed, it would nevertheless be significant if we could show that the electorate had become more ideologically polarized and more likely to vote on the basis of ideology. Because of the continued plurality of conservatives over liberals, such a behavioral change would greatly benefit the Republicans and could have important long-term implications.

Given the evidence presented on candidate polarization in the previous chapter, there is good reason to expect that liberals and conservatives might be more sharply divided in the 1980s than previously. One way of testing this is to examine how liberals and conservatives rate their own group as opposed to the other ideological camp. For example, if those who placed themselves as strong conservatives were to rate "liberals" lower on the feeling thermometer than in the past and "conservatives" higher, then this would be an important sign that ideological polarization had indeed taken place.

Table 5.2 compares the relationship between self-placement positions and feeling thermometer ratings in 1988 to that found in 1972. Rather than increasing, the differences between ratings of "liberals" and "conservatives" in fact declined slightly. In almost every instance conservative and liberal identifiers became less favorable toward their own ideological group and more favorable toward the other group. And moderates in 1988 more truly reflected a centrist position, as their average preference for "conservatives" was roughly half that of 1972. Overall, this table shows a decrease rather than an increase in ideological polarization.

Finally, the relationship between the vote and liberal/conservative placements must be examined for evidence of greater ideological polarization. Given the long-standing co-

Table 5.2 Mean feeling thermometer ratings by ideological
self-placement, 1988 and 1972

	Conservatives	Liberals	Difference
1988			
Strong conservatives	74.3	37.2	+37.1
Weak conservatives	65.3	48.9	+16.4
Moderates	59.1	54.6	+4.5
Weak liberals	54.3	60.4	−6.1
Strong liberals	46.3	66.6	−20.3
1972			
Strong conservatives	76.6	37.3	+39.3
Weak conservatives	68.2	45.4	+22.8
Moderates	61.9	53.0	+8.9
Weak liberals	53.1	65.3	−12.2
Strong liberals	45.4	76.1	−30.7

Source: CPS National Election Studies.

alition between Republicans and conservative southern
Democrats, American party politics has traditionally been
less oriented around left-right placements than European
politics. Ever since the days of Roosevelt's attempted purge
of conservative Democrats in 1938, talk of realignment has
often centered on the possibility of a more ideologically
based voting pattern. Thus, if it could be shown that ideology has come to play a larger role in voting behavior, we
would have an important sign of fundamental change in the
party system.

Once again, however, the data do not support this hypothesis. The data presented in Table 5.3 show that Carter

Table 5.3   Republican percentage of the two-party vote by ideology, 1972–1988

	1972	1976	1980	1984	1988
Strong conservative	90.2	81.8	82.5	85.3	85.4
Weak conservative	84.6	73.6	70.0	77.7	67.1
Moderate	68.9	47.5	60.6	55.0	48.7
Weak liberal	43.7	26.9	40.5	33.1	23.2
Strong liberal	17.2	15.8	7.9	22.6	10.1

Source: CPS National Election Studies.

Note: If the Anderson vote is included in 1980, we get the following figures (from top to bottom): 79.5, 63.6, 54.1, 33.7, 6.7.

won in 1976 by doing better than McGovern had in 1972 among weak liberals and moderates, and that he lost his presidency to Reagan primarily because of his inability to hold on to these same two groups. Although the number of conservatives in the electorate increased from 1976 to 1980, the Republican percentage of the two-party vote among strong and weak conservatives remained virtually unchanged. In contrast, the Republican vote among moderates and weak liberals increased by over 10 percent. Thus, somewhat paradoxically, the key ideological factor in 1980 was Carter's inability to maintain his electoral base among the two groups to whom his views were closest on the left-right scale. It is quite ironic that the election that produced the most ideological change in public policy in recent memory was also probably the least determined by liberal/conservative preferences in the electorate.

The 1984 data reveal a somewhat stronger impact of ideology on the vote, but nothing unusual relative to other figures in the short time period for which data are available. Although Reagan identified himself as a conservative more than any recent president, it is interesting to note that Nixon actually garnered 5 percent more of the conservative vote in 1972. The 1988 figures also match previous patterns, and indeed are virtually identical to the 1976 figures. One might infer that the small increase in conservatives was enough to tip the election results in the Republicans' direction, but this is not the case. Ford actually won 52.8 percent of the vote among those who could place themselves on the ideology scale in 1976, versus 54.0 percent for Bush in 1988. The difference was that Bush maintained the same margin among those who did not think of themselves in ideological terms, whereas these non-ideological voters gave Carter the edge he needed to win in 1976.

In sum, the data on ideological preferences reveal neither a shift toward conservatism of any great magnitude nor an increase in the relationship of ideological preferences to the vote. This is an important contradiction of the Schatt-schneider argument that elections act as a general guide for public policy, indicating preferences for either more conservative or liberal policies.

Changes in Specific Policy Preferences

Much evidence demonstrates that ideological orientations are far from perfectly correlated with specific policy preferences.[8] It is thus possible that major shifts to the right on individual policy questions were of great importance in presidential voting during the 1980s, despite the absence of fundamental ideological change.

The number of policy questions on which time series data are available for the last several elections is regrettably rather limited. Many important policy debates of the 1960s and 1970s, such as Vietnam and urban unrest, are no longer relevant, whereas others like Central America and cutting taxes

Table 5.4 Policy attitudes, 1964–1988 (in percents)

	1964	1968	1972	1976	1980	1984	1988
Power of the federal government							
Too powerful	30	41	41	49	50	32	34
Not too powerful	36	30	27	20	15	23	20
No opinion	34	29	32	31	35	45	47
Pace of civil rights actions							
Too fast	66	65	48	41	36	31	26
About right	27	29	43	49	51	56	59
Too slow	6	7	9	9	14	12	16
Aid to minorities							
Help themselves	—	—	43	44	49	37	46
In-between	—	—	23	22	29	31	24
Govt. should help	—	—	35	35	22	32	30
Jobs policy							
Each person on own	—	—	45	49	49	44	50
In-between	—	—	23	21	21	23	21
Govt. should help	—	—	31	30	31	34	28
Role for women							
Place is in home	—	—	31	26	21	17	15
In-between	—	—	20	20	17	24	17
Equal role	—	—	49	55	62	60	69
Health insurance							
Private insurance	—	—	40	43	—	42	39
In-between	—	—	14	12	—	21	19
Govt. plan	—	—	46	44	—	38	42

Table 5.4 (Continued)

	1964	1968	1972	1976	1980	1984	1988
Busing							
Favor	—	—	10	10	10	8	—
In-between	—	—	5	7	6	8	—
Oppose	—	—	86	82	84	84	—
Abortion							
Never permit	—	—	11	11	10	—	—
Permit if health in danger	—	—	47	46	45	—	—
Permit if personal difficulty	—	—	17	17	18	—	—
Permit in all cases	—	—	25	27	28	—	—
Never permit	—	—	—	—	12	13	13
Permit if rape/incest/health	—	—	—	—	33	30	33
Permit if other clear need	—	—	—	—	19	20	19
Personal choice	—	—	—	—	37	36	36

Source: SRC/CPS National Election Studies.

Note: Question wording can be found by consulting NES codebooks. For 1988 the variable numbers are as follows: power of the federal government = V5804; pace of civil rights action = V5801; aid to minorities = V639; jobs policy = V622; role for women = V726; health insurance = V617; abortion = V734.

are specific to the 1980s. Fortunately, the NES has made an effort to develop some general questions on economic and social policy issues, which are applicable to changing circumstances. The data from these questions are displayed in Table 5.4 and demonstrate changes in *both* liberal and conservative directions.

The only clear indication of movement toward the right concerns what may be the most important general domestic policy issue of our time—the size of the federal government. When this question was first asked in 1964 more people felt that the government was not too powerful than felt the opposite. But after the rapid expansion of federal programs following the 1964 election a notable backlash occurred against the scope of activities emanating from Washington. This proved to be a substantial advantage for Nixon in 1968 as well as in 1972—so much so that no Democratic nominee since has run on a platform of bigger government. Ronald Reagan may have been the first president to cut the growth rate on domestic spending, but Jimmy Carter's 1976 campaign perfected the strategy of running for head of the federal establishment by railing against it.

With candidates of both parties favoring a smaller government, the nature of this issue changed markedly. In 1976 and 1980 both Democratic and Republican identifiers were more likely to feel that the government was too powerful than the opposite. Once something was actually done to reduce the rate of growth of domestic spending, however, the percentage who felt that government was too big declined substantially. Still, Walter Mondale—the political heir to the Humphrey legend—carefully avoided advocating renewed federal expansion in 1984, stating at the Democratic convention that his platform contained "no laundry lists that raid our treasury."

The question of government power has indeed taken on many of the characteristics of a valence rather than a position issue. In 1984 and 1988 the difference in presidential voting behavior between those with opposing points of view on the government power question was less than 1 percent. This compares to a difference of 53 percent in 1964. In sum, there has been a distinct transformation in public opinion on this crucial question, but it is one which the party system has adapted to rather than been reshaped by.

For a time in the late 1960s and early 1970s it was generally thought that social issues, involving equal rights, abortion, and various matters related to the counterculture movement, would be the major driving force in any realignment.[9] Such policy stands played a large part in distinguishing the Reagan administration from its predecessors. Reagan was widely viewed as being less favorable toward the civil rights movement than any president in the last generation. His nomination saw the Republican Party reverse its long-standing support for the Equal Rights Amendment, and his administration became the first openly to oppose affirmative action since it was put into effect under Lyndon Johnson.

These policy reversals, however, did not correspond to any rightward shift on social issues. Issues like busing and abortion are so deeply rooted that little change is to be expected, and indeed none can be found. Others like civil rights and women's place in society reflect a slow process of changing values in favor of greater equality of opportunity. For example, on the role of women in running business, industry, and government, there has been a gradual liberalization, resulting in a 20-percent increase in the percentage of respondents favoring an equal role for women. Similarly, feeling thermometer ratings of the "women's liberation movement" increased from an average score of 46 in 1972 to 55 in 1984, and after ratification of the Equal Rights Amendment failed in 1982 more people expressed disappointment than pleasure with the outcome.

Turning to the question of civil rights more generally, since 1964 respondents have become increasingly satisfied with the pace of civil rights leaders' actions. Whereas two-thirds of the public thought the pace was too fast in 1964, barely a quarter believed this to be the case by 1988. Of course this is in part due to the actual slowing of the civil rights movement, but it is probably safe to say that it involves a gradual acceptance of the movement as well. Feeling thermometer ratings of "civil rights leaders" indicate an increase in positive affect from a mean rating of 41 in 1972 to 58 in 1988.

In recent years the focus of the civil rights movement has shifted from questions of equal opportunity to problems of economic inequality. Although the Reagan administration sharply cut specific programs aimed at these goals, the survey data indicate very little, if any, change in public opinion about the programs. The NES question that asks whether the government in Washington should make every effort to improve the social and economic position of blacks and other minorities provides a good general measure of these attitudes. Between 30 and 35 percent of those with an opinion have consistently favored government assistance for minorities. The only exception to this general finding is 1980, when the proportion in favor of minority aid dropped markedly. But this was probably due to the experimental change in question wording with this item in 1980. This involved adding the phrase, "even if it means giving them [blacks and other minorities] preferential treatment" to the description of government aid. By making this indirect reference to affirmative action policies, it seems likely that the marginals on the question would be altered in the conservative direction. Once this phrase was removed in 1984, the results returned to their previous stable pattern.

Two other elements of stability in policy attitudes are federal health insurance and full employment programs. The public has been virtually evenly split since 1972 on whether a national health care plan should be adopted. Federal action on jobs has been somewhat less popular, with roughly a third consistently favoring government action "to see to it that every person has a job and a good standard of living," while about half have chosen the conservative option. The fact that the marginals on both this and the minority aid question have been consistently skewed against government action could possibly be interpreted as indicating that support for Reagan's domestic spending cuts existed long before his election. Given the general nature of the questions, however, the conservative tilt of the responses may merely reflect Americans' preference for relying on self-help whenever possible rather than vocal opposition to economic aid programs already in place.

The available survey data on attitudes toward domestic spending indicate that the latter interpretation is more plausible. Respondents in 1980 were asked to place themselves on a scale with one end representing the position that government should provide fewer services in order to reduce spending, and the other representing the position that government services should be maintained. Only 33 percent of those with an opinion wanted a decrease in spending compared to 47 percent who wanted to maintain government services at current levels, with 20 percent at the in-between point. In 1984 and 1988 more balanced wording was adopted and the question asked about cutting versus increasing social service spending. Despite the fact that the only politician advocating an increase was Jesse Jackson, slightly more people favored spending increases over decreases in both years.

When one turns to specific areas of government expenditure there are even stronger indications of public support for continued growth throughout the 1970s and 1980s. It has often been said that Americans are ideological conservatives but operational liberals—meaning that they oppose the idea of big government in principle but favor it in practice. The general questions discussed thus far tap much of the conservative government values. In contrast, the data displayed in Table 5.5 on attitudes toward spending for specific programmatic areas tap the operational liberal side of American opinion. Here, one can see that the public has consistently

Table 5.5　Attitudes toward government spending, 1961–1988

	1961	1969	1974	1976	1978	1980	1982	1983–1984	1986	1988
Welfare	+46	+7	−21	−49	−47	−45	−29	−23	−18	−19
Military	+47	−23	−25	−3	+6	+48	−1	−11	−24	−23
Foreign aid	−52	−71	−76	−75	−67	−68	−67	−69	−63	−63
Space	−7	−51	−55	−53	−38	−23	−28	−26	−30	−17
Blacks	—	—	+11	+2	−1	0	+8	+13	+18	+19
Education	—	—	+44	+42	+42	+44	+48	+56	+56	+60
Environment	—	—	+55	+47	+45	+34	+38	+48	+54	+60
Health	—	—	+61	+57	+51	+49	+50	+52	+55	+63
Crime	—	—	+65	+61	+61	+66	+67	+62	+59	+64
Big cities	—	—	+46	+26	+23	+21	+23	+27	+28	+36
Social security	—	—	—	—	—	—	—	+42	+50	+47
Assistance to the poor	—	—	—	—	—	—	—	+51	+52	+61

Source: 1961, 1969: Philip Converse et al., *American Social Attitudes Data Sourcebook, 1947–1978* (Cambridge, Mass.: Harvard University Press, 1980); 1974–1988: NORC General Social Surveys.

Note: Figures represent the percentage of each sample indicating the government is spending too little minus the percentage indicating the government is spending too much. Data for 1983 and 1984 have been combined because only a randomized third of the 1984 sample were asked these questions. Differences between the 1983 and 1984 samples appear to be minor, nevertheless.

favored more government spending in areas such as education, the environment, health, fighting crime, and aiding economically troubled big cities. The public has also generally been slightly more in favor of than opposed to expenditures to improve the economic condition of blacks, with some evidence of increasing support after the Reagan budget cuts.

Only on programs without an established constituency—foreign aid and the space program—has there been continuing public desire for spending cuts.

The two items that show noteworthy change in Table 5.5 are welfare and defense. Interestingly, in 1961 the idea of a trade-off between "guns and butter" did not exist in the public mind, with a large plurality favoring greater government spending on welfare as well as defense. However, as welfare spending grew as the result of the Great Society programs, and military spending rose to support the Vietnam War, public support for both declined. By the time Nixon entered the presidency, there existed only a slight edge in favor of increased welfare spending, and the balance of opinion on defense spending had shifted toward budget cutting. But while opposition to more military spending leveled off, attitudes toward welfare turned increasingly negative as politicians of both parties attacked its seeming wastefulness. It was Carter, after all, who said repeatedly in 1976 that the country's welfare system was a "disgrace." As Tom Smith has shown, the term "welfare" has developed negative connotations of help for "loafers and bums." Smith argues that attitudes toward spending for "assistance to the poor" is a much better measure for support for the welfare state;[10] and as can be seen at the bottom of Table 5.5, most people favored increased spending when this wording was used. Thus, at best one could say that Reagan, like Carter before him, had a mandate to cut waste in welfare—not to dismantle redistributive policies.

In contrast, the data on military spending offer the one solid significant change in public opinion that may have contributed to a shift in the vote in 1980. The increase in support for defense spending from 1978 to 1980 is the largest two-year shift recorded in Table 5.5. This rapid rise in support for military spending apparently occurred as events in Iran and

Afghanistan threatened American prestige abroad. In the absence of a foreign crisis or war, most citizens pay scant attention to international relations. Therefore, when dramatic events such as the Iranian hostage crisis and the Soviet invasion of Afghanistan take place, public opinion can be rapidly swayed one way or the other, as in fact happened in 1980. The fact that support for increased defense expenditures quickly waned after Reagan took office indicates just how superficial and transitory such feelings were. Indeed, there was never any indication of an increase in pro-militaristic feelings in the public, as evidenced by the stability of feeling thermometer ratings of the military. Nor was there widespread support for Reagan's views on getting tough with the Russians, with only 36 percent in 1980 agreeing, whereas 39 percent thought we should try hard to get along with them, and 24 percent placed themselves somewhere in between.

As with the data on ideological preferences over time, the public's stance on specific issues does little to confirm the notion that Reagan was swept into office by a rightward swing in public opinion. Furthermore, while the data on ideology indicate a consistently higher level of support for the conservative label, on specific policy questions there are more cases in which the balance of opinion went against the conservative stance than vice versa.

Candidate Policy Proximities

The most precise way of assessing the existence and magnitude of policy mandates is to compare voters' positions with their perceptions of the candidates' positions. To construct these measures of policy proximity, absolute value distances between a respondent's position on the seven-point scales and his or her perception of each of the candidates must be obtained. This information is then used to determine which of the candidates the respondent feels closer to, if either.

This technique has the advantage of providing information beyond merely the voter's stand on the issue. It also has the disadvantage of being subject to various psychological processes of rationalization. It has often been argued that voters may project their feelings about a candidate onto their perception of where he stands on the issues, thereby distorting the candidate's true position.[11] For example, in 1980 the widespread feeling that Carter had been a "weak" president led many to conclude that he was against increased defense spending when his public statements were clearly to the contrary.

The problem of rationalization has led some scholars to disregard the public's perceptions of candidate policy stands. Shanks and Miller, for instance, chose not to use the data because of their "conviction that proximity of 'true' perception measures represent an unidentifiable combination of relative proximity and a variety of other performance and candidate-related determinants."[12] It is true with regard to 1980 that perceptions of Carter's stands were subject to much rationalization, thus making Reagan appear closer to the public on policy issues. But the 1984 and 1988 data shown in Table 5.6, are more instructive. On most of the policy questions more people perceived the Democratic nominee to be closer to their own position than Reagan. That the Republicans nevertheless won these elections—especially the landslide election of 1984—strongly indicates the lack of influence of policy considerations.

There are three possible explanations: (1) that policy proximities were important to the vote decision in 1980 but heavily discounted in 1984 and 1988; (2) that they had relatively little impact in any of the elections; or (3) that in 1980 people felt it necessary to rationalize their responses to con-

Table 5.6 Proximity to party leaders on policy scales, 1980–1988 (percentage of respondents placing themselves closer to the Republican than to the Democrat)

Reagan vs. Carter	Winter 1980	Spring 1980	Summer 1980	Fall 1980
Defense spending	+1	+10	+19	+23
Get along with Russia	−2	+7	+13	+17
Government services	−2	−3	+9	+7
Inflation-unemployment	+10	+15	+19	+8
Aid to minorities	—	+7	+21	+22
Government job programs	—	+9	—	+16
Federal tax cut	—	—	—	+7
Abortion	—	—	—	−12
Equal role for women	—	—	—	−25

Reagan vs. Mondale	Winter 1984	Spring 1984	Summer 1984	Fall 1984
Defense spending	−25	−26	−22	−16
Get along with Russia	—	−14	−5	−5
Government services	−4	−6	0	−3
Central America	—	−32	−32	−23
Aid to women	—	−3	+4	−2
Aid to minorities	—	—	—	−3
Government job programs	—	—	—	+3

	Reagan vs. Dukakis Fall 1988	Bush vs. Dukakis Fall 1988
Defense spending	−16	−6
Get along with Russia	−6	0

Table 5.6   (Continued)

	Reagan vs. Dukakis Fall 1988	Bush vs. Dukakis Fall 1988
Government services	+9	+7
Aid to minorities	−8	+1
Aid to blacks	−9	0
Government job programs	−3	+6
Equal role for women	−25	−18
Health insurance	—	−1

Source: 1980 NES P1, C1, P2 and C3-C3PO datasets; 1984 NES Continuous Monitoring Study for Winter thru Summer and NES Pre-Post data for Fall; 1988 NES Pre-Post Study.

Note: Question wording can be found in NES codebooks. For 1988 the variable numbers are as follows for the self-placement questions: defense spending = V609; get along with Russia = V707; government services = V601; aid to minorities = V639; aid to blacks = V631; government job programs = V622; equal role for women = V726; health insurance = V617.

form with their vote choice, whereas in 1984 and 1988 they did not. The answer is probably some mixture of all three, but I believe the third explanation makes the most sense. The guiding theory, simply stated, is that when voters are voting an incumbent out of office, they have a strong need to rationalize their choice and establish cognitive balance, whereas this need is much weaker when they are satisfied with the incumbent.

To test this theory, it is especially valuable to have data from several points during the campaign in order to trace the possible adjustment of perceptions to match candidate preferences. Table 5.6 presents data from four time points in 1980 and 1984 indicating the proportion of the population closer to Reagan on each policy question minus the proportion closer to the Democratic candidate. There appears to be some movement toward greater proximity to Reagan as both the 1980 and 1984 campaigns progressed, but the trend is far more evident for 1980.

Hypothetically, Reagan's increasing proximity advantage during the 1980 campaign may have been due to changes in public sentiment, or changes in perceptions of either Reagan's or Carter's positions. Unlike the essentially stable public preferences one finds on the policy scales during 1984, there was a good deal of movement in the electorate's views in 1980. However, in five out of six cases (government services being the exception) the public actually moved in a *liberal* direction during the 1980 campaign. (This is not shown in the table.) Considering that any change in the perception of Reagan's stand was toward a more conservative viewpoint, it is puzzling that more people actually considered themselves closer to Reagan's policies as the campaign progressed. The answer to this seeming enigma is that public perceptions of Carter moved toward the liberal side much more than did public attitudes. For example, on defense spending the mean score for the electorate moved from 5.3 to 5.2 between winter and fall, whereas the mean perception of Carter's stand went from 4.7 to 3.7.

What is especially revealing about this pattern is that Carter's public statements over the campaign year were surely in a more conservative than liberal direction. On foreign policy it was particularly clear that the international crises had convinced President Carter of the necessity of a defense buildup, and that the Soviet invasion of Afghanistan had turned him toward a harder line against the Russians. Nevertheless, these are the two most notable cases of the electorate perceiving a liberal drift in Carter's position.

One possible explanation for this phenomenon is that early perceptions of Carter may have been framed by how he compared to Kennedy, whereas after the conventions Reagan's stands would have become the appropriate reference point. In other words, Carter might have looked considerably more liberal when compared to Reagan in the fall than he seemed when compared to Kennedy during the first half of the year. But if this were the case, one would expect to find a similar pattern with Mondale as he moved beyond the battle with Hart and Jackson to the contest with Reagan. There is only the slightest evidence of this in 1984, however. The mean perception of Mondale on the defense spending question, for example, moved only one tenth of a point in the liberal direction during the course of the 1984 campaign.

Unlike the 1980 campaign, when Carter actually led Reagan by a substantial margin during the winter and stayed close until the very last week, Mondale was consistently far behind Reagan in the polls throughout 1984. Thus, the crucial difference seems to be that in 1980 voters needed to rationalize the Democratic candidate's policy stands to conform with their change in vote intention. This is most clearly shown by the 1980 NES panel data, in which four interviews were conducted with the same respondents over the course of the year. The panel data confirm the hypothesis that most of the change in the perception of Carter's policy positions can be traced to people who shifted their candidate preference from Carter to Reagan. For example, between the initial survey contact in the winter and the pre-election interview in October, Democrats who ended up defecting changed their perception of Carter on the defense spending scale from a mean of 4.8 to 3.5. By comparison, those who remained loyal to the Democratic ticket saw little change in Carter's position on defense, with mean placements of 5.1 in the winter and 4.9 in the fall. A similar pattern of change also occurred on the question of Soviet relations and the trade-off between unemployment and inflation.

In short, it appears that Reagan gained an advantage on policy questions during the 1980 campaign not because people shifted to a more conservative set of policy preferences, but because many felt it necessary to rationalize their perception of Carter in order to vote against him. This rationalization did not occur to any significant degree in 1984 because voters decided early on to support the incumbent *in spite of their differences with him on policy questions*. Knowing what the results of Reagan's period in office had been, many voters in 1984 apparently felt safe in just discounting the importance of these differences.

Similarly, while the 1988 election can be considered a positive referendum on the Reagan administration, it cannot be said to be an endorsement of his policies. As can be seen in the last segment of Table 5.6, on six of the seven policy questions that were asked in 1988 more people preferred their perception of Dukakis's stand to Reagan's. The fact that Bush was perceived as more moderate than Reagan proved to be an asset rather than a liability. While Dukakis's stands were seen more favorably than Reagan's, Bush's were seen as equally preferable to the Democratic candidate. Bush enjoyed an edge in terms of proximity on the issues of government services and job programs, whereas Dukakis had an advantage in the areas of defense spending and women's roles. The four other survey questions showed a virtually even split in terms of policy proximity to the nominees. Again, the 1988 data show little sign that even a plurality of the public desired more conservative policies.

Open-Ended Policy Comments

One possible general criticism of the data presented above is that the findings are necessarily limited to the topics for which questions were specifically asked. There may be other policy questions of great importance to the vote. In 1984, for example, the question of raising federal income taxes—as proposed by Walter Mondale—was inexplicably not addressed in the otherwise comprehensive interview schedule. Yet, if the political pundits agreed that the 1984 election settled any single policy dispute, the tax increase question was it.

Fortunately, the open-ended questions concerning the candidates allow respondents to define what they think are the most important issues relevant to their vote decision. Although the coding of these responses is often not as precise as would be desired, it is possible to identify frequently mentioned responses that seem likely to reflect policy attitudes.[13] Tables 5.7, 5.8, and 5.9 present the major policy responses to open-ended questions about the candidates in 1980, 1984, and 1988.

As was the case with the closed-ended data on policy attitudes, there is little in these tables to indicate a mandate for Reagan's program. Again, the best case can be found on the question of defense spending in 1980. This was the most salient policy reason for voting for Reagan (mentioned by 6.1 percent) as well as the most frequently stated reason for voting against Carter (3.7 percent). Other matters that drew a noteworthy number of comments were tax cuts and government spending (each mentioned by 3.6 percent of those interviewed), and the women's issues of the Equal Rights Amendment and abortion—which as with the proximity measures were Reagan's greatest policy weaknesses in 1980.

Overall, however, it is striking how little policy concerns figured in people's responses about what they liked and disliked about Carter and Reagan in 1980. It is particularly amazing that no single policy stand of the incumbent drew a positive response from even 1 percent of the public, and only four did so on the negative side. Similarly, policy reasons

Table 5.7   Open-ended policy reasons for voting for or against
Reagan and Carter in 1980

For Reagan because of:		*Against Reagan because of:*	
Strong military position; pro-Pentagon spending	6.1%	Opposition to ERA	3.0%
		Anti-abortion stance	2.0%
Support for lower taxes	3.6%	Too much military spending	1.8%
Conservative ideology	2.9%		
Opposition to government giveaways	1.2%	Conservative ideology	1.5%
		Opposition to government aid	1.1%
		Social security cuts	1.1%
For Carter because of:		*Against Carter because of:*	
No reason given by more than	1%	Weak military stand; Pentagon cuts	3.7%
		Excessive government spending	3.6%
		International policy (meddles in others' problems)	1.7%
		Policy allowing influx of refugees	1.3%

Source: CPS National Election Study.
Note: Only responses given by more than 1 percent of the population
surveyed are included.

for voting for Reagan were scarce, and these were evenly
counterbalanced by negative comments on other policies.

For 1984 the salience of policies in the open-ended responses was much higher—both in terms of the frequency of
comments and the sheer range of policies mentioned. What
is particularly noteworthy about the 1984 open-ended comments, though, is that negative comments far outweigh posi-

Table 5.8 Open-ended policy reasons for voting for or against Reagan and Mondale in 1984

For Reagan because of:		*Against Reagan because of:*	
Strong military position; pro-Pentagon spending	9.8%	Opposition to social security	9.0%
Support for lower taxes	4.7%	Too much military spending	6.7%
Loose monetary policy	3.1%	Opposition to aid for the elderly	4.2%
Anti-abortion stance	3.1%		
Opposition to government activity	2.3%	Opposition to welfare spending	3.9%
Conservative ideology	1.9%	Tax reform policy (supports loopholes)	3.8%
Opposition to welfare	1.9%		
Support for school prayer	1.6%	Opposition to government activity	3.2%
		Insufficient aid to education	2.4%
		Opposition to detente with Soviet Union	2.3%
		Anti–nuclear freeze stance	1.9%
		Failure to separate church and state	1.8%
		Tax policy (unspecified)	1.3%
		Anti-abortion stance	1.2%
For Mondale because of:		*Against Mondale because of:*	
Support for government activity	2.1%	Policy of higher taxes	8.5%
Pro–nuclear freeze stance	1.9%	Pro-abortion stance	2.9%
Support for social security	1.8%	Weak military policy	2.7%
Support for income tax reform (opposes loopholes)	1.8%	Support for government activity	2.5%
		Support for welfare programs	2.5%

Table 5.8 (Continued)

For Mondale because of:		Against Mondale because of:	
Support for lower taxes	1.1%	Liberal policies	2.0%
		High government spending	1.6%

Source: CPS National Election Study.
Note: Only responses given by more than 1 percent of the population surveyed are included.

tive ones for *both* candidates. It is true that policy responses have historically been more likely to be negative than performance or candidate attribute responses, but the negativity of the policy remarks in 1984 is unprecedented.[14] At best, Reagan's advantage was that he represented the lesser of two evils.

Specifically, the only policy area where the open-ended data show evidence for a Reagan mandate is on the tax increase issue. This was by far the most frequent reason voters gave for being against Mondale and the second most salient reason for voting for Reagan. Thus the pundits were right in saying that Reagan's promise not to increase taxes was a definite advantage for him in the 1984 election. His promise was important not only because it was popular, but also because Reagan's track record made it believable. In contrast, Reagan's other major promise—not to cut social security—was met with much skepticism. Nine percent spontaneously said they disliked Reagan because he would reduce social security and another 4 percent expressed dislike of his lack of support for aid to the elderly. In the end, the public's doubts about Reagan's commitment to social security turned out to be somewhat justified given his 1985 proposal to postpone the scheduled cost of living increase.

Table 5.9 Open-ended policy reasons for voting for or against Bush and Dukakis in 1988

For Bush because of:		*Against Bush because of:*	
Strong military position; pro-Pentagon spending	5.7%	Too much military spending	3.2%
Anti-abortion stance	4.5%	Arms sales to Iran	3.2%
Conservative ideology	2.7%	Diversion of money to Contras	2.5%
Support for lower taxes	2.2%		
Support for the death penalty	1.7%	Opposition to abortion	1.8%
		Opposition to social security	1.4%
For Dukakis because of:		*Against Dukakis because of:*	
Support for aid to education	2.9%	Lenient policy toward criminals	8.9%
National health insurance policy	2.5%	Pro-abortion stance	7.0%
Support for welfare/ poverty programs	2.4%	Weak military position; defense spending cuts	4.4%
		Liberal ideology	4.3%
Support for active government	1.8%	Support for higher taxes	4.3%
Pro-abortion stance	1.2%	Opposition to death penalty	3.6%
		Support for gun control	2.5%
		Support for active government	2.4%
		Lenient policy toward polluters	1.9%
		National health insurance policy	1.2%

Source: CPS National Election Study.
Note: Only responses given by more than 1 percent of the population surveyed are included.

As was the case in 1980, Reagan's support for a military buildup was the most frequently stated policy reason for voting for him. In 1984, however, such comments were largely counterbalanced by negative remarks about excessive military strength and the desire for a nuclear freeze. Nevertheless, the open-ended responses on defense spending were far better for Reagan than the results from the seven-point scales. Apparently those who cared most about the question were more favorable to increased spending than the general population.

A final interesting note on the 1984 data concerns the centerpiece of the Reagan administration's 1985 and 1986 agenda—tax reform. Ironically, this topic elicited a fair amount of negative comments from people who felt Reagan would not support tax simplification. Such a phenomenon is the unfortunate result of a presidential campaign that eschews commitments to future actions, as did Reagan's 1984 campaign. Rather than risk support on a promise that might divide his constituency, Reagan chose instead to make only the vaguest of commitments to tax reform, which scarcely anyone paid attention to. As a consequence of this lack of information concerning Reagan's plans, attitudes on the question were improperly translated into the vote decision in 1984.

The 1988 Bush campaign emulated this style of eschewing policy commitments. Rather than discussing what policies he would pursue, Bush focused on sensationalizing issues that were damaging to Dukakis, such as the Willie Horton furlough. From the open-ended data in Table 5.9 one can see that the Bush strategists were successful in tagging Dukakis with a whole series of unpopular stands and actions. Most salient was the perception that he was weak on crime, as emphasized in the infamous revolving-door commercial. Although Dukakis tried to counter by saying that he would be tough on crime, more people criticized him as weak on the issue than commented negatively on Mondale's open proposal for a tax increase in 1984. While mentioned only half as much as in 1984, the issue of higher taxes also hurt Dukakis, despite his careful ambiguity on the matter. The big difference between 1984 and 1988 can be seen in the dramatic increase in negative remarks about the Democrat as a liberal, for abortion, and against defense spending. No doubt the strong Bush rhetoric accounts for most of this, as well as for putting Dukakis's stands against the death penalty and for gun control on people's minds.

In short, the 1988 open-ended data supply good evidence of the effectiveness of negative campaigning. The Bush campaign was far more successful in saddling the opposition with negative policy images than it was in creating a positive image about the course Bush would pursue. As with Reagan in 1980, Bush was elected to office in 1988 with relatively few salient policy images—either positive or negative. Perhaps the most important question in 1988, though, was not so much what people thought Bush and Dukakis might do, as how the public evaluated Reagan's policies after nearly eight years.

A 1988 Retrospective on Eight Years of Reagan Policies

In the 1988 election study respondents were asked a series of questions on whether spending on federal programs had increased, stayed the same, or decreased since Reagan took office. Those with an opinion were then asked whether they approved or disapproved of this course of action. These data are presented in Table 5.10, the first section of which reveals a distressingly low level of public information about the redirection of federal policy. Despite the dramatic changes in

Table 5.10 Perception and approval of government policy actions during the Reagan years (in percents)

	Increased	Stayed the same	Decreased	Don't know
Federal programs since 1981				
Efforts to protect the environment	24.1	27.6	20.9	27.4
Social security benefits	42.0	21.7	16.0	20.3
Defense spending	70.0	6.8	3.4	19.8
Assistance to the poor	20.4	26.4	27.5	25.7
Spending on public schools	23.4	24.9	21.9	29.7
Approval by those with opinion				
Efforts to protect the environment	93.4	27.5	8.1	
Social security benefits	94.5	29.4	4.3	
Defense spending	50.3	55.0	32.8	
Assistance to the poor	78.0	31.5	17.1	
Spending on public schools	83.6	22.0	10.1	

Source: 1988 CPS National Election Study.

presidential priorities, the survey results show a startling lack of knowledge about how spending had been cut on assistance to the poor, public schools, and the environment. Less than 30 percent of those interviewed were able to say that spending had been reduced in each of these areas. In fact, slightly more people thought that spending on public schools and environmental protection had increased.

On social security and defense spending, however, public perceptions were much clearer. Forty-two percent of the public thought that social security benefits had increased compared to just 16 percent who thought they had been reduced. Yet, it should be noted that Reagan had relatively little impact upon social security, regularly yielding to the Democratic majority in the House of Representatives. Only in the area of national defense was a majority of the public able to perceive a change in government priorities attributable to Reagan. Of the 80 percent who said they had paid some attention to the matter, seven of eight respondents correctly said that defense spending had increased. Thus, if the Reagan years truly represented a revolution in public policy, the public itself was only cognizant of this one aspect.

Another unique aspect of the Pentagon spending issue concerns the relationship between citizens' perception of the policy change and their approval of it. Of the great majority who believed that defense spending had increased, half approved and half disapproved. Many people thus knew what had occurred, and opinions of the change were equally divided. In contrast, on all the other issues those who perceived spending increases overwhelmingly voiced approval whereas those who perceived cuts overwhelmingly disapproved. Even on assistance to the poor only 17 percent of the respondents who thought there had been cuts approved of them.

It is no wonder that Bush painted himself as the "education President" and an environmentalist in 1988. Had the public seen the Reagan cuts in these two areas as clearly as they saw the increases in defense spending, such actions would clearly not have been well received. In the end, only 2 percent of the public *knew and approved of* spending cuts on education and the environment; ten times as many people expressed approval of the spending increases they erroneously believed to have occurred. In sum, the 1988 survey data fail to show an after-the-fact mandate for many of Reagan's policies on federal spending. The electorate was evenly polarized on defense increases, and generally unaware and unsupportive of domestic cuts.

Of course, these spending issues were not the only policy areas on which the Reagan administration made a mark. For example, the hard-line policy against communism also figured prominently in the Reagan agenda. By turning to open-ended questions one can assess the salience and popularity of a wider range of policy actions. Adapting the standard open-ended questions about the candidates to the situation of a retiring president, the 1988 election study asked people whether there was anything in particular they liked and disliked about what Reagan had done as president. Paralleling the responses to the closed-ended questions, the results, shown in Table 5.11, reveal more disapproval than approval for Reagan's policy actions.

It is interesting that the most frequent positive statement was that Reagan pursued detente with the Soviet Union. As with Nixon's trip to China, Reagan's past stand on communism gave him the credibility to garner support for détente across the ideological spectrum when the opportunity presented itself. Indeed, liberals were slightly more likely to praise Reagan's pursuit of detente than conservatives. Therefore, these comments can hardly be interpreted as an endorsement of Reagan's conservative approach to government.

The only evidence of support for more conservative policies can be found on the issue of defense spending. Nearly 10 percent said they liked Reagan's "pro-Pentagon" position compared to about 5 percent who complained about

Table 5.11 Open-ended policy reasons for liking or disliking the Reagan administration, 1988

Like Reagan because of:		*Dislike Reagan because of:*	
Support for detente with Soviet Union	10.4%	Arms sales to Iran	5.4%
Strong military position; pro-Pentagon spending	9.6%	Too much military spending	4.7%
		Support for Contras	3.4%
Cautiousness on government spending	1.8%	Opposition to social security	3.3%
Support for social security	1.7%	Insufficient aid for education	3.0%
		Diversion of money to Contras	2.4%
		Lenient policy toward polluters	2.2%
		Opposition to active government	2.2%
		Opposition to welfare/ poverty programs	2.0%
		International policy (meddles in others' problems)	1.1%
		Excessive foreign aid	1.0%

Source: CPS National Election Study.

Note: Only responses given by more than 1 percent of the population surveyed are included.

excessive military spending. This matches the finding from 1984 that people who were most concerned with this issue were more supportive of the defense buildup than the general population (as measured by responses to closed-ended questions).

Consistent with other findings are statements of dissatisfaction with cuts in domestic spending—particularly in areas like education and the environment. And on social security twice as many people criticized Reagan's actions as praised them. Finally, the open-ended data indicate that Reagan's decisions to sell arms to Iran and support the Contras were quite costly in terms of public support, contributing substantially to the net disapproval of his policy actions.

The idea of a policy mandate is no doubt an inherently difficult concept to test empirically. Each campaign brings many issues to light, and an individual's vote can hardly be considered an expression of support for an entire multi-faceted program. Walter Lippmann made this point effectively in *The Phantom Public*: "We call an election an expression of the popular will. But is it? We go into a polling booth and mark a cross on a piece of paper for one of two, or perhaps three or four names. Have we expressed our thoughts on the public policy of the United States? Presumably we have a number of thoughts on this and that with many buts and ifs and ors. Surely, the cross on a piece of paper does not express them."[15] Thus, to expect widespread public support for all of Reagan's policy stands is certainly to expect too much.

Yet the general pattern uncovered in this chapter indicates that the marginal shift in the vote had little to do either with the major policy changes Reagan and Bush proposed or with any rightward shifts in public opinion. Although much has been made in the popular press about the increasingly conservative mood of the electorate, the data presented here demonstrate a high degree of stability. On political ideology the shift to the right was minimal. Specific policy questions show some small changes in both liberal and conservative directions, and the only indication of a mandate is the rapid rise in public support for more defense spending that occurred in 1980. Taking measures of policy proximity to the candidates, Reagan did have an advantage on most policies in 1980, but this seems to have largely resulted from people rationalizing their decision to support him by moving Carter's position further away from their own. By 1984 and 1988 the situation was reversed with more people actually closer to the Democratic candidate and apparently just discounting the importance of their policy differences with Reagan. Responses to the open-ended questions concerning policy matters were relatively absent from dicussion in 1980 and were largely negative toward both candidates in 1984. Finally, assessing the eight years of the Reagan presidency, the public had more negative than positive comments to make about Reagan's policies, and closed-ended questions indicate no after-the-fact mandate for changes in federal spending.

Given the data from the previous chapter on candidate popularity and findings in this chapter on policy issues, we might wonder how the lopsided Republican victories of the 1980s could have occurred. Was the electorate acting irrationally in electing conservative Republican presidents for three consecutive terms? The following chapter on performance issues shows how policy judgments were quite rationally overriden during the 1980s.

SIX

Performance-Based Voting

As argued in Chapter 1, the focus of the candidate-centered age has increasingly been on short-term results—primarily economic in nature. Rightly or wrongly, presidents are now viewed as being responsible for solving, or failing to solve, the nation's current political problems.[1] Regardless of whether their policies have an effect or not, presidents receive more of the credit and the blame for the country's immediate condition. Given this greater focus on short-term results, when policy preferences conflict with performance assessments, the latter are increasingly likely to take precedence in voting decisions.

Indeed, a key to understanding the presidential elections of the 1980s is to recognize that many voters were torn between the candidate they thought would adopt the best policies and the candidate they thought would perform better. Political observers and commentators all too often assume that people have perfectly consistent attitudes. It is often inferred that any candidate who wins by a large margin is widely popular and supported on policy questions. Political scientists, in contrast, have long been aware of the fact that mass political attitudes are often inconsistent. Attitudes on complex public policy issues scarcely exist for many people, and survey responses can often be better understood as "non-attitudes."[2] Thus, journalists may mistakenly assume that attitudes are consistent, whereas survey researchers may be quick to write off conflicting attitudes as superficial.

A recent contribution to the academic literature by John Zaller, however, starts from the idea that "most people do not possess single fixed attitudes toward most political issues, but instead possess sets of frequently conflicting considerations."[3] Zaller thus points to the possibility of contradictory attitudes being a natural and meaningful part of political life. His theory calls for a variety of "response axioms" to demonstrate how people transform these multiple attitudes into survey responses.

For the purposes of this chapter what is necessary is to develop a comprehensive explanation of how incongruous results on policy and performance measures were resolved in the Republicans' favor during the 1980s.

Theories of Performance-Based Voting

The question "What have you done for me lately?" has long been part of the colloquial terminology in describing the rise and fall of party fortunes.[4] But until recently performance assessments had been largely unstudied in the voting behavior literature. This scholarly neglect stemmed in large part from the fascination with testing the assumptions of traditional democratic theory. Furthermore, the tendency to regard performance voting as unsophisticated and readily apparent probably led early investigators to give such factors short shrift. In a new empirical field it is understandable that the pioneers would neglect the seemingly obvious, no matter how important it might prove to be.

Indeed, the early election studies paid scant attention to the role of performance, as evidenced by the few haphazard

questions uncovered by Morris Fiorina in his review of retrospective voting measures.[5] It was not until 1968, for example,
that a variant of the standard Gallup question on presidential
approval was introduced to the election studies. Similarly,
the 1968 presidential election study was the first in which
respondents were asked about the success of the national
economy over the past year. Given the nature of the elections
of the 1950s, it would be hard to argue that neither approval
of the job the president had been doing nor the state of the
national economy were important factors. But on the basis of
the survey data from the 1950s, these factors cannot be demonstrated in any direct way.

In *The American Voter* performance assessments were addressed only indirectly through an analysis of the open-
ended questions about the parties and candidates. People
who focused on performance considerations such as peace
and prosperity were placed in the category of ideological
sophistication labeled "nature of the times," which ranked
second-lowest in sophistication (above the group identified
as demonstrating "no issue content"). Respondents in this
category, according to *The American Voter*, act as "a rather
crude and insensitive thermometer geared to the goodness and
badness of the times."[6] Campbell and his coauthors describe
their behavior pattern as follows: "If they perceive that times
have been hard, as symbolized primarily by economic dislo-
cation or war, they will react in a spirit of 'throwing the
rascals out.' If they perceive that times have been relatively
good, the tendency will be to adopt a 'don't rock the boat'
attitude."[7] The authors leave little doubt about how they
interpret such behavior, writing that the "rascals" phrase
was chosen quite deliberately, as "it makes minimal assumption as to the sophistication of the actor."[8] Thus, one can
readily extend the interpretation to conclude that policy alternatives make little impact on these voters. In fact, the authors

state that "the salient fact is that the party in power has failed in its most basic obligations, and deserves to be turned out. Protest can be bitter without a breath of program behind it."[9]

By concentrating so narrowly on measuring voter sophistication, *The American Voter* largely failed to address the possible functions of performance-based voting—for the political system and the individual. These functions have been prime areas of concern for many analysts virtually ever since, however. Rational choice theorists have particularly focused on the lowered information costs associated with performance (as opposed to policy) evaluations. Given the public's limited attentiveness to politics, these theorists argue that it is quite sensible for most voters to pay more attention to results than to means. Fiorina puts this best when he states that citizens "typically have one comparatively hard bit of data: they know what life has been like during the incumbent's administration. They need *not* know the precise economic or foreign policies of the incumbent administration in order to see or feel the *results* of those policies."[10] In other words, performance-based voting offers people a reasonable shortcut for ensuring that unsuccessful policies are dropped and successful policies continued.

Of course, one counterargument is that policies may be reversed as seeming failures when in fact they had little to do with subsequent developments. When Campbell and his coauthors referred to "nature of the times" voting as being "crude and insensitive," this is no doubt part of what they had in mind. Nevertheless, a recurring theme in the recent literature is that what is important is merely that electoral reward and punishment be dispensed—regardless of whether the policies and the outcomes are truly connected. Benjamin Page, for example, writes that "even if the Great Depression and lack of recovery were not at all Hoover's fault . . . it could make sense to punish him in order to sharpen the

incentives to maintain prosperity in the future." Acknowl-
edging that blame may be placed unfairly, he notes, "To err
on the side of forgiveness would leave voters vulnerable to
tricky explanations and rationalizations; but to err on the
draconian side would only spur politicians on to greater en-
ergy and imagination in problem solving."[11] Therefore, what
is crucial is that voters have a target for their blame when the
government falters in some respect.

As Key wrote in *The Responsible Electorate*, "The only really
effective weapon of popular control in a democratic regime is
the capacity of the electorate to throw a party from power."[12]
Like other proponents of retrospective voting, Key believed
that candidates and parties must be held generally account-
able for the state of the economy and the country's foreign
affairs during their time in office. Although democratic theory might indicate that voters should base their decisions on
the stated policy aims of the candidates, to do so without
regard to the actual governmental results could be counter-
productive according to Key's logic. Does it make sense, for
instance, to pay much attention to the positions of an ineffective administration that seemingly cannot make good on its
promises and program? Retrospective voting theorists, such
as Key, would undoubtedly answer no—as did the 1980 electorate. Similarly, is it logical to vote an administration out of
office for unpopular policy stands if the overall results are
perceived positively? Again, the theory of retrospective voting would say no, and so did the electorate in 1984 and 1988.

Presidential Performance Evaluations, 1980–1988

The evidence that wide majorities disapproved of Carter's
job performance and approved of Reagan's is quite clear, as
displayed in Table 6.1. Approval or disapproval of the way
the incumbent "is handling his job as president" has been

Table 6.1   Presidential job approval ratings, 1980–1988

Carter, 1980	Inflation	Unemployment	Iran	Overall
Strongly approve	7.0	10.7	15.7	13.4
Approve	16.3	20.3	15.4	27.1
Disapprove	24.7	25.5	11.9	22.2
Strongly disapprove	52.0	43.6	48.2	37.3

Reagan, 1984	Economy	Foreign affairs	Overall
Strongly approve	31.2	27.1	35.3
Approve	27.0	25.3	28.1
Disapprove	15.0	15.0	15.1
Strongly disapprove	26.8	32.6	21.5

Reagan, 1988	Economy	Foreign affairs	Overall
Strongly approve	25.7	30.9	33.2
Approve	28.3	30.1	26.6
Disapprove	17.1	15.4	15.2
Strongly disapprove	28.9	23.6	25.0

Source: CPS National Election Studies.

strongly tied to the vote on the individual level, most notably in 1984 when 87 percent of those who approved of Reagan's handling of his job voted for him compared to only 7 percent of those who disapproved. As shown by Richard Brody and Lee Sigelman, one can predict election outcomes quite well by presidential job approval ratings.[13]

The results from this general presidential approval item are quite consistent with the theory of retrospective performance voting. Carter's high disapproval rate in 1980 showed public sentiment for "throwing the rascals out," whereas

Reagan's high approval ratings in 1984 and 1988 indicated a generalized satisfaction with how things were going. Yet, as noted in Chapter 4, this question is not terribly useful when it comes to drawing meaningful conclusions about the *nature* of presidential support. To approve of a president's job performance is not to say, "My president, right or wrong." In particular, the preceding chapter demonstrated that Reagan's policy stands were more often a liability than an asset.

Just the reverse was the case with performance assessments, however. As with the review of policy measures in the previous chapter, it is informative to examine the content of the open-ended questions for the salience of specific kinds of performance-related statements. These data demonstrate the high degree of consensus that existed on questions of performance as opposed to those of policy.

A comparison of the performance responses for 1980, displayed in Table 6.2, with the policy responses given earlier (see Table 5.7) confirms that the former were far more common as reasons for voting against Carter. Although the generic responses presented in each table are limited to those that were mentioned by more than 1 percent of the population, they do encompass the large majority of all such comments. It is therefore noteworthy that of these comments the performance reasons for disliking Carter outnumbered the policy reasons by a three-to-one ratio. On the other hand, although there were no policy reasons mentioned by more than 1 percent for liking Carter, two performance comments easily passed this threshold. The fact that both of these concerned foreign relations indicates the disapproval of Carter was centered on economic questions, in spite of the Iranian fiasco and public desire for increased defense spending. Similarly, the few salient performance comments regarding Reagan in 1980 were all oriented toward the economy on the

Table 6.2   Open-ended performance reasons for voting for or against Reagan and Carter in 1980

For Reagan because:		*Against Reagan because:*	
The times will be better under him	3.6%	Chance for peace would be poorer	6.8%
He won't increase the national debt	3.6%		
Inflation will be less	2.2%		
Wages will be higher	1.9%		
For Carter because:		*Against Carter because:*	
Chance for peace would be better	5.1%	He handled the Iranian crisis poorly	12.4%
He handled the Iranian crisis well	3.3%	Inflation has been worse	6.2%
		Times have been worse economically	4.5%
		He hasn't produced any results	2.5%
		He has handled trouble spots poorly	2.3%
		Unemployment has been worse	2.2%

Source: CPS National Election Study.
Note: Only responses given by more than 1 percent of the population surveyed are included.

positive side, while on the negative side it was frequently mentioned that Reagan might reduce the chance for peace. As a challenger Reagan presented an image of someone who would take strong action to preserve American prestige, but many worried that his actions might be *too* strong.

In 1984, as shown in Table 6.3, performance comments were actually somewhat less prevalent in the open-ended

Table 6.3   Open-ended performance reasons for voting for or against Reagan and Mondale in 1984

For Reagan because:		_Against Reagan because:_	
The times are good; general conditions better	10.4%	He has handled the budget deficit poorly	4.3%
Wages have been better	5.8%	Chance for peace would be worse	3.1%
Inflation has been lower	5.4%	Wages have been worse	3.0%
He is generally doing a good job	3.2%	He has handled Russia poorly	1.2%
He has been good for the U.S.	3.1%	The times are bad; general conditions worse	1.2%
Chance for peace would be better	1.4%	He has handled trouble spots poorly	1.0%
For Mondale because:		_Against Mondale because:_	
Unemployment will be better under him	3.2%	No reason given by more than	1%
He won't increase the national debt	2.8%		

Source: CPS National Election Study.
Note: Only responses given by more than 1 percent of the population surveyed are included.

data than policy comments. But while policy issues were quite salient in evaluations of Reagan in 1984, only 40 percent of such comments were positive. This compares to a figure of 70 percent positive for the frequently mentioned performance codes, which for Carter in 1980 was a lowly 22 percent.

The change is most visible on economic matters. Whereas Carter drew criticism in 1980 for the perception that wages and inflation had gotten worse, these subjects drew positive remarks for Reagan in 1984. If one tries to explain the change in the incumbent's share of the vote from 1980 to 1984, the open-ended data thus point to assessments of presidential performance (primarily economic) as the answer. Yet, as D. Roderick Kiewiet and Douglas Rivers have noted, the key difference was not so much the overall performance of the economy as the point in the business cycle when the election occurred. In their words, "The economy under Reagan followed a pattern that was, in terms of the president's political interest, nearly optimal. The economy under Carter, in contrast, looks like a political business cycle run backwards."[14]

Similarly, the 1988 outcome can best be interpreted as a positive referendum on the results of the Reagan presidency. In Chapter 5 we saw that when asked to say what they liked and disliked about the Reagan presidency in 1988, respondents gave more negative policy comments than positive ones. And in Chapter 4 it was shown that comments about Reagan's personal attributes—particularly his competence— were also skewed in the negative direction by 1988. However, when it comes to performance criteria, there was a wealth of positive comments, as revealed in Table 6.4. Aside from some discontent about the national debt, Reagan drew overwhelming praise for the results of his administration. As in 1984, many of the comments centered on the good economic news. People may not have wanted to see social services cut, but they were very pleased with low unemployment and low inflation. Furthermore, by 1988 Reagan was being praised not only for prosperity but for peace as well. Although the majority opposed aid for the Contras or further defense increases, they welcomed the progress on arms control and the lessening of tensions with the Soviet Union.

In sum, if short-term results are indeed more important in the candidate-centered age, as argued in Chapter 1, then it is

Table 6.4   Open-ended performance reasons for liking or disliking
the Reagan administration, 1988

Like Reagan because:		Dislike Reagan because:	
The times are better (economic prosperity)	9.6%	He has handled the national debt poorly	7.8%
Wages/salaries are better	7.7%	He has handled trouble spots poorly	1.2%
He has handled Russia well	6.5%		
There is a better chance for peace	6.2%		
Inflation is lower	6.1%		
He has made people feel good about America	5.8%		
He has done a good job	3.8%		
He has raised American prestige	3.5%		
He has handled terrorism well	2.9%		
He has united Americans	1.5%		

Source: CPS National Election Study.
Note: Only responses given by more than 1 percent of the population
surveyed are included.

no wonder that the Republicans won the elections of the
1980s. But what do performance measures really mean, and
can they in fact be separated from policy attitudes?

Establishing the Meaning of Performance Measures

One common criticism of the measures employed to measure
presidential performance is that they are so vague as to leave
open a variety of possible interpretations. It could be argued,
for example, that when people indicate they approve of how

a candidate has handled the economy, what is meant is they favor his stands on taxes, social services, and government jobs programs. Similarly, when respondents make open-ended statements to the effect that the president has done a good job in keeping the United States out of war, this may mean they favor his program for military buildup, which in turn is seen as responsible for ensuring the peace. In other words, perceptions of a president's policies may be the primary basis upon which voters decide whether they approve of his performance.

Such a decision process seems reasonable when recent policy actions can easily be tied to important governmental results. For instance, one can make a plausible argument that approval of Nixon's handling of the economy in 1972 hinged on his implementation of wage and price controls earlier in the year. Likewise, support for Nixon's policy decisions to pursue détente with China and the Soviet Union no doubt greatly affected ratings of his job on foreign affairs. If the public can attribute the results to the policy choices, then performance measures may be interpreted as support for policies as well as results. After all, policies do inevitably produce results of one sort or another.

This theoretical framework can be found most prominently in the work of Warren E. Miller and J. Merrill Shanks on the 1980 and 1984 elections.[15] Miller and Shanks analyze voting patterns using a multistage statistical process in which policy attitudes are specified as influencing the vote both directly and indirectly, via their role in shaping performance evaluations. The intellectual roots for such an analysis can be traced back to the "funnel of causality" concept in *The American Voter*.[16] This concept was devised to illustrate the point that forces which are relatively proximal to the vote are heavily influenced by more enduring factors further removed from the vote decision.

The advantage of employing the "source-oriented" perspective according to Miller and Shanks is that the analyst can look forward "toward the vote decision from the given variable's position, and emphasize its total effect on the vote."[17] Applied to the question of the relative importance of policy versus performance, Miller and Shanks make a good case for performance evaluations being more temporally proximal to the vote. Certainly policy attitudes are usually less subject to sudden variations and therefore more likely to be enduring from election to election. What is questionable, though, is whether policy stands exert a substantial direct influence on performance assessments—as they assume. This seems plausible in the above example regarding 1972, but for the elections of the 1980s such a causal flow hardly seems likely.

Indeed, for 1980 a good argument can be made for performance attitudes shaping policy attitudes rather than vice versa. For example, given the events of 1980, it is hard to imagine how attitudes on defense spending could account for the slide in Carter's job approval. In early 1980 the rally-round-the-flag phenomenon gave Carter some of the highest approval ratings of his term. His approval rating on foreign affairs plummeted only after it became clear that the Iranian crisis would not be swiftly resolved and that Carter was unable to deter the Soviets from invading Afghanistan. If anything, presidential performance in this instance led to adjustments in policy opinions, as frustrations with America's seeming weakness led many to support increased defense spending. Miller and Shanks thus vastly overestimate the impact of policy attitudes in this case by specifying military spending opinions as influencing the vote because of its correlation with presidential approval.

Similarly, with the precipitous economic decline of 1980, it seems unlikely that many people actually felt excessive government spending and taxation were much to blame for the high inflation, unemployment, and interest rates. If this were the case, we would have to assume a much deeper level of thought about (or a much greater degree of interest in) policy alternatives and actual results than the average voter exhibits. It seems far more plausible to argue that the poor state of economic affairs made voters receptive to a change in policy direction, or alternatively to a new candidate with little regard for policy considerations.

From this perspective, policy attitudes can be seen as reflecting possible solutions to short-term problems, with the nature and severity of the problem guiding the receptiveness to new alternatives. Once the problem appears to be resolved, support for the policy approach may quickly dissipate. Indeed, the case of defense spending illustrates just such a chain of events, as delineated in the previous chapter. If, however, the public had continued to support Reagan on defense beyond the initial military buildup, this would have indicated the establishment of a long-term commitment to such a conservative posture.

Even then, it would still be a risky assumption to infer that such basic values necessarily influence performance assessments *independent of* actual results. The social welfare programs of the New Deal, for example, came to be seen favorably by much of the public as they proved to be successful. It is doubtful that the degree to which Roosevelt's successors endorsed such programs determined how people evaluated their performance in terms of the economy. Except for particular groups such as blacks and the poor, who feel most sharply affected by economic policies, the results will usually take precedence over the means in determining approval ratings on the economy.[18]

To say that policy usually had little effect on voters' assessments of performance should not be read as implying that basic value priorities have no effect whatsoever on the vote. A more sensible alternative model is to presume that people vote on the basis of *both* what they believe is "the right thing to do" and the perceived success of what has been done. In short, what is most questionable about the Miller-Shanks model is their assumption that what voters believe is right necessarily affects how successful the president is thought to be.

The crucial case of 1984 provides ample evidence for the argument that people voted for Reagan for what he had accomplished, while at the same time holding reservations about his policy initiatives. If judgments on how the president is handling his job can indeed be traced to policy stands, then it simply does not follow that Reagan could be evaluated positively on the former and negatively on the latter. The only logical explanation for this pattern is that to the extent that both actual results and policy options influenced presidential job approval, the results clearly predominated.

The 1984 NES data provide an excellent set of questions to test this thesis. Table 6.5 presents a series of equations predicting respondents' approval of Reagan's handling of the economy and foreign affairs. For economic approval the policy predictors are the questions concerning the level of social services and government-guaranteed jobs programs; the performance predictors are the questions of whether the national economy and the respondent's personal finances have been better or worse over the last year. For predicting approval of the president's handling of relations with other countries, there are three available policy measures (defense spending, detente with the Soviet Union, and intervention in Central America) and two measures of performance (which party would be most likely to keep the peace and perceived changes in the strength of the U.S. position in the world). By employing a linear regression model to determine the rela-

Table 6.5   Regression equations predicting 1984 job approval measures

	Beta	T stat
Predicting Reagan's handling of the economy from:		
National economic situation	.47	24.5
Personal financial situation	.15	7.8
Social service spending	.15	8.0
Government guaranteed jobs	.10	5.4
(N = 2046)	R = .63	
Predicting Reagan's handling of foreign affairs from:		
Party best for peace	.34	17.2
U.S. position in the world	.30	16.2
Central America involvement	.10	5.5
Detente with Russia	.09	5.5
Defense spending	.09	4.6
(N = 2037)	R = .64	

Source: CPS National Election Study.

Note: "Don't know" and "haven't thought about it" responses on the independent variables have been recorded to the middle point in order to preserve as many cases as possible for analysis.

tive weight of these factors on the two respective job approval items, the focus is deliberately on the extent to which policy stands exert an independent influence upon job approval.

The standardized coefficients displayed in Table 6.5 suggest that there is very little influence indeed. Job ratings of Reagan's handling of the economy were clearly dominated by judgments of whether national business conditions had improved, stayed the same, or worsened over the past year (beta = .47). As to be expected from recent research regarding sociotropic voting,[19] the effect of how people viewed the change in their family's economic situation was much less by comparison. Equally marginal, though, were the policy issues of spending on social services and government-guaranteed jobs. And on approval of Reagan's handling of foreign affairs a similar pattern of results greatly outweighing policies can be found. In this case both of the result-oriented measures have coefficients of .30 or above, whereas all three of the foreign policy coefficients are limited to .10 or less. In sum, these equations illustrate that the direct effect of policy stands on presidential job approval items was rather limited in 1984, controlling for measures of government results.

Similar conclusions can be drawn from 1988 approval ratings of how Reagan had handled his eight years in office. As discussed in the previous chapter, respondents were asked whether they approved or disapproved of various changes in federal policies during Reagan's time in office. Added to these variables in the regression equation in Table 6.6 are questions asking whether the economy, national security, and the budget deficit had gotten better, worse, or stayed the same over the last eight years. Again, performance assessments clearly outweighed policy factors in determining job approval. Given that people were most aware of changes in defense spending, it should not be surprising to find that this was the most significant policy issue in terms of predicting Reagan's job approval. However, it pales compared to the performance variables of the state of the economy and national security. Not all performance factors were of great importance, though. Interestingly, while the state of the economy and national security were very significant, the budget deficit was not. People apparently cared little about a balanced budget as long as the state of the nation remained healthy. One could hardly imagine a more ideal weighting of the variables for Reagan. The two items on which people were largely positive—the economy and national security—

Table 6.6 Regression equation predicting approval of Reagan's handling of the presidency

	Beta	T stat
Over the last eight years _____ has gotten better, worse, or stayed the same:		
the economy	.32	14.6
national security	.33	15.0
the budget deficit	.06	3.1
Approve or disapprove of changes in federal _____		
efforts to protect the environment	.09	5.0
social security benefits	−.02	−1.0
defense spending	.13	6.3
assistance to the poor	.10	5.1
spending on public schools	.04	2.1
(N = 1536)	R = .71	

Source: 1988 CPS National Election Study.

Note: "Don't know" and "haven't thought about" responses on the independent variables have been recoded to the midpoint in order to preserve as many cases as possible for analysis.

were of prime importance, whereas the budget deficit and unpopular policy actions were discounted.

Translating Policy and Performance into Candidate Evaluations

If policy and performance assessments in fact produced conflicting attitudes throughout the 1980s, then using the two together to predict the vote should reveal only that one factor dominated over the other. A more sophisticated explanation would be that each had a substantial impact on candidate evaluations—one on positive attitudes and the other on negative attitudes—with either the former or the latter being weighted more in the final decision. In other words, it may be that Republican policies had a large effect on people's reservations about their candidates, but that positive performance elements were more strongly related to the vote. With a model predicting a simple summary measure (such as feeling thermometer ratings or the vote) it is impossible to test such a hypothesis. It is therefore necessary to have separate measures of positive and negative feelings to assess fully what role policy and performance judgments played in the formation of candidate evaluations. Such distinct measures are available in the NES survey data in the form of the answers to the candidate like and dislike questions, which will be employed as separate dependent variables in this section.

Whether the electorate votes more negatively or positively has been discussed in both the popular press and the academic literature, with the common wisdom being that negative opinions exert disproportionate influence. As Curtis Gans, the director of the Committee for the Study of the Electorate, writes: "Our political marketplace increasingly is becoming one in which voters are asked to say no: against Barry Goldwater in 1964, against Lyndon B. Johnson in 1968, against George McGovern in 1972, against the Watergate excesses of Richard M. Nixon in 1974 and '76, against Jimmy Carter in 1980 and against Walter F. Mondale in 1984."[20] No doubt he would add against Michael Dukakis and Willie Horton in 1988.

In a similar vein, political scientist Samuel Kernell notes that "recent research in social psychology largely complements the view that negative opinions exercise disproportionate influence in political behavior."[21] From this, he develops a theory of negative voting to explain partly the usual loss of seats suffered by the president's party in the off-year election. His basic finding is that those who disapprove of the job the president has done are more likely to turn out than those who approve of him, thereby disadvantaging the party's candidates. "To the degree that negative evaluations are more determinative than positive ones, even a popular president may prove to be a net liability to his party's congressional candidates," Kernell concludes.[22]

However, the minimal research which has been done on this question should hardly be taken as a definitive case for negative voting. Few data have been brought to bear on the question, and rarely have the data been well designed to address the problem. It is quite telling that when surveys have asked people whether they were voting mainly for a candidate or against his opponent, most respondents said they were making a positive choice. The National Election Studies reveal that in the 1960 Kennedy-Nixon contest 85 percent claimed to be voting for a candidate rather than against one, and in the 1964 Johnson-Goldwater race 69 percent classified themselves as positive voters. Similarly, when the *New York Times*/CBS News poll asked this question in 1976, 1980, and 1988, positive voters outnumbered negative voters by at least 10 percent.[23]

More useful for establishing general patterns of electoral behavior, as well as for revealing specifics about the elections of the 1980s, are the like/dislike data. As shown in Table 6.7, the number of likes about the Democratic and Republican candidates has consistently explained more variance in the two-party vote than the number of dislikes toward either party's candidate.[24] This finding holds true for elections in which both candidates have been well liked, such as the Eisenhower and Stevenson contests, as well as for recent elections in which the candidates have been far less popular.

Table 6.7 Regression equations predicting the two-party vote from positive and negative statements about the candidates

	1952	1956	1960	1964	1968	1972	1976	1980	1984	1988
# of likes about the Republican	.33	.35	.39	.44	.43	.25	.28	.27	.37	.32
# of likes about the Democrat	−.28	−.30	−.26	−.20	−.29	−.29	−.29	−.34	−.37	−.33
# of dislikes about the Republican	−.17	−.22	−.15	−.15	−.12	−.23	−.19	−.15	−.12	−.15
# of dislikes about the Democrat	.17	.10	.16	.19	.12	.23	.23	.25	.16	.21
R	.65	.68	.72	.74	.73	.68	.67	.69	.75	.72

Source: SRC/CPS National Election Studies.
Note: Entries are standardized regression coefficients and multiple correlation coefficients. Positive coefficients indicate that as the variable increases the likelihood of a Republican vote also increases.

Therefore, contrary to the popular wisdom, the like/dislike data provide excellent evidence for the conclusion that American voters cast their ballots with a focus more on the positive than on the negative.

Yet one should not interpret this finding as indicating that the net unpopularity of candidates such as Goldwater and McGovern were of little importance. Rather, these data should be seen as suggestive of a more complex argument that weak candidates suffer more than anything else from their failure to inspire reasons for voting for them. In other words, the fact that the Goldwater candidacy struck so few positive chords with the public was more important in explaining the variance in the vote than the fact that his candidacy provoked so many negative comments.[25]

Why positive factors are more important than negative factors in the vote decision is a question that goes well beyond the scope of this book. Perhaps because democracy allows citizens freedom of choice, they are more likely to feel that they are making a positive choice, rather than merely settling for preventing the worst. In any case, the pattern displayed in Table 6.7 leads to an interesting interpretation of the open-ended questions. Positive comments can be seen primarily as justifications for voting for a particular candidate. In contrast, negative comments often reflect a substantial percentage of mere reservations that run contrary to the respondent's vote intention. Such lingering negative doubts are probably easier to discount than are positive reasons that might attract a voter to the opposing candidate.

Turning to the data in Table 6.7 from the 1980s, it is interesting to note that the reasons given for voting against Jimmy Carter in 1980 were more important in explaining the vote than the negative comments regarding any other candidate. Thus the Carter candidacy suffered not only from the high degree of negative evaluations but also because such liabilities were more directly related to the vote than at any time since the election studies began in 1952. In contrast, Reagan's 1984 reelection campaign also provoked numerous negative comments (see Chapter 4), which the regression data show were remarkably unrelated to the vote. The coefficient of −.12 for the dislikes of Reagan in 1984 is the smallest for any incumbent in the time series. Furthermore, the .37 coefficient for positive comments about Reagan is the highest such figure for any of the six incumbents. Compared to other incumbents, Reagan's 1984 situation was therefore an ideal one of having his positive features accentuated and his negative features minimized.

As might be expected from the patterns displayed thus far, positive attitudes about Reagan and Bush were mostly determined by performance, whereas the less important negative attitudes were more policy oriented. This can be seen in the analysis displayed in Table 6.8. For each year a summary measure of policy opinions was constructed from approximately fifteen questions encompassing stands on economic,

Table 6.8　Regression equations predicting positive and negative comments about the candidates from policy and performance indices

1980	Likes of Reagan	Dislikes of Reagan	Likes of Carter	Dislikes of Carter
Presidential performance	−.31	.09	.37	−.46
Policy positions	−.16	.23	.13	−.04
R	.38	.27	.42	.47

1984	Likes of Reagan	Dislikes of Reagan	Likes of Mondale	Dislikes of Mondale
Presidential performance	.51	−.35	−.37	.30
Policy positions	.09	−.23	−.25	.14
R	.56	.49	.53	.38

1988	Likes of Bush	Dislikes of Bush	Likes of Dukakis	Dislikes of Dukakis
Presidential performance	.36	−.25	−.28	.29
Policy positions	.17	−.19	−.22	.17
R	.44	.35	.40	.37

Source: CPS National Election Studies.
Note: Table entries are standardized regression coefficients and multiple correlation coefficients.

foreign, minority aid, and social issues by subtracting the number of liberal responses from conservative responses.[26] Summary measures of performance were created by calculating means from the job approval items on the economy and foreign affairs found in Table 6.1. These questions, as demonstrated above, are primarily result-oriented and therefore represent the best possible operationalization of the concept of presidential performance available in all three elections.

In all but one case, the standardized regression coefficients displayed in Table 6.8 indicate that performance outweighed policy in predicting the number of likes and dislikes about the candidates. Interestingly, this exception occurred with regard to reasons for voting against Reagan in 1980. Thus, people used Carter's lackluster performance as a justification for voting for Reagan while at the same time expressing misgivings about Reagan's policy stands.

Judgments of President Carter's performance in 1980 were naturally highly related to reasons for voting both for and against him. Given the preponderance of disapproving responses, it is not surprising that we find a higher coefficient for predicting the number of negative comments. What is most significant, however, is the virtually nonexistent impact of policy positions in shaping the public's dislikes of Carter. This offers further support for the thesis that Carter was thrown out of office for his perceived failure to solve governmental problems rather than for his approach to them.

In fact, policy stands were actually more consequential in explaining why people liked Carter than why they disliked him. This was even more true for the Mondale candidacy in 1984—as is consistent with the general argument that his policy stands were closer to more of the electorate than Reagan's. Also in line with this theme is the strong relationship between policy positions and the number of reasons for voting against Reagan in 1984. As with the 1980 data, however, policy positions were greatly outweighed by performance factors in explaining the variance in positive attitudes toward Reagan.

Reagan thus had multiple advantages in how evaluations concerning him were translated into the vote during his reelection bid. Assessments of his performance were predominately favorable. Furthermore, they were highly related to the positive reasons citizens expressed for voting for him, which in turn were more determinative of the actual vote than ever before for an incumbent seeking reelection. In contrast, the electorate was far less supportive of Reagan on policy questions, and his policies were the primary reasons people voted against him, although policy issues were less related to the vote than at any time in the last three decades.

One possible conclusion from this chapter's analysis is that Reagan's electoral victories were extraordinarily lucky. Many voters held contradictory attitudes toward him, but time and again, the data show, they were largely resolved in his favor. Factors that were to Reagan's advantage were invariably emphasized in the voting decision, whereas those to his disadvantage were minimized.

To attribute all of this to luck, however, is to ignore a very clear pattern: both the closed-ended and open-ended data show that judgments of presidential success in producing desirable economic results were primarily responsible for shifts in the vote. If there is anything particularly lucky about this, it is most likely that factors beyond either president's control, such as the price of oil, led to a recession in 1980 and an economic upswing from 1983 to 1988. In the candidate-centered age, when presidents are widely viewed as responsible for the economic health of the country, what would be truly lucky is if a president were to win in spite of unfavorable economic indicators. It is noteworthy that Carter attempted to do just this in 1980 by running against Reagan's policy statements more than on his own record. Although he was successful in making policy stands a major factor in reasons for disliking Reagan, they were only weakly translated into the vote decision. Indeed, the public was closer to the Democratic nominee than to Reagan on most policy questions throughout the 1980s, but this Democratic advantage was vastly overshadowed by positive assessments of Reagan's performance on the economy and foreign relations.

The Republicans managed to avoid the old campaign manager's axiom, "policy issues can't help you but they sure can kill you." Extremist candidate that he was, Reagan could well have been defeated under circumstances in which policies played a much larger role in the decision-making process, either directly or indirectly via their effect on performance judgments. These circumstances did not exist largely because policy and performance assessments were relatively incongruent. Given this disparity, the ends clearly outweighed the means by which they might be pursued.

SEVEN

The Impact of Candidate-Centered Politics

Nowhere is the impact of what Anthony King has labeled "the new American political system"[1] more evident than in the changes that have occurred in patterns of electoral behavior since the election of John F. Kennedy in 1960. As the electoral process has changed since 1960, so has American political behavior. In the immediate aftermath of the 1988 election, a comparison with that of 1960 illuminates many of the major changes discussed in this book.

The 1960 and 1988 Elections Compared

At first glance, the 1988 and 1960 elections would appear to be quite similar. Both involved choosing a successor to a two-term Republican president with high overall approval ratings; and in both instances the incumbent vice president faced a relatively unknown Democrat from Massachusetts running with a prominent senator from Texas. In fact, one could easily have taken the 1960 cast of characters and placed them into comparable roles for 1988. Yet, with the transformation from party politics to candidate-centered campaigning, it would have been much like casting Shakespearean actors in the frantic chases and slapstick comedy of the 1963 hit movie "It's a Mad, Mad, Mad, Mad World."

One of the most obvious differences between 1960 and 1988 has been touched upon at various points in this book—the dramatic changes in the presidential nomination process. What was once a relatively straightforward task conducted largely out of public view has been transformed into a long and tortuous media circus. In the 1960s the nomination battle was essentially a test of a candidate's ability to build support among the small cadre of party leaders; in the 1980s building a constituency among primary and caucus voters throughout the fifty states has become the key test.

In contrast to the primary marathon faced by Michael Dukakis in 1988, there were only two primary contests that drew any attenion in 1960—West Virginia and Wisconsin. All told, Kennedy's primary victories (mostly in uncontested races) produced just 18 percent of the delegates he needed for the nomination. These victories were more important in convincing party leaders that Kennedy had popular appeal than anything else. Kennedy won few delegates in West Virginia, for example, but he soon picked up several key endorsements as a result of this victory. In this sense, the 1960 nomination can be seen as a transitional one from leadership choice to popular choice. Yet, had the party leaders turned against him—as they did against Kefauver in 1952—Kennedy would probably have been defeated.

Not only has the nomination process been opened up by the proliferation of primaries since 1960, the caucuses are now public events as well. This is most evident in Iowa, where massive efforts are focused on mobilizing grass roots support in the nation's first test of candidate strength. Even the most important contest of the 1960 nomination race, the West Virginia primary, merited only ten days of Kennedy's time. In 1988 Iowa loomed so large that nearly a thousand candidate days were spent there, with some candidates going so far as to rent apartments in Des Moines. Compare this to the start of the 1960 campaign in New Hampshire, where Nixon did not even campaign and Kennedy was opposed only by Paul Fischer—a ballpoint pen executive from Chicago who ran a campaign on the then revolutionary idea of flat tax rates.[2] While Dukakis made much out of the notion that he was following in Kennedy's footsteps by winning in New Hampshire, the 1960 contest is little more than a footnote in the history books. Indeed, that is exactly what Theodore White gave it in *The Making of the President, 1960*.[3]

On the Republican side, there is no comparison between the hard path that George Bush had to travel and Richard Nixon's 1960 campaign. By the standards of the candidate-centered age, Nixon's road to the 1960 nomination was a breeze. The only Republican who even considered running against him was Governor Nelson Rockefeller of New York, who tested the waters in late 1959, found that the party's leaders were solidly behind Nixon, and never went beyond toying with the idea of challenging him. Bush, by contrast, was challenged in the primaries by five strong opponents: Dole, Kemp, Haig, Robertson, and Du Pont.

Because the parties no longer exercise control over the selection of presidential nominees, their command over the voters' attention has lessened considerably. As shown in Chapter 2, voters have not only increasingly said that they vote for the man rather than the party; they have actually done so with great frequency. In 1960 Kennedy just managed to win with the help of the Democratic advantage in party identification. In contrast, the Bush victory in 1988 had relatively little to do with blind party loyalty.

Rather than a 1960 rerun, the 1988 election ended up as a come-from-behind victory reminiscent of 1948. Bush, like Truman, initially suffered by comparison to his predecessor.

As election day approached, though, the patterns which had governed political behavior for nearly two decades reasserted themselves in favor of each man. In Truman's case the relevant pattern was the New Deal coalition and the overriding importance of partisanship. In 1988, Bush benefited not from a reassertion of partisanship but from the fact that party ties are now so weak.

Since 1960, party dealignment has made it far more difficult for a party which is divided in the spring and summer to unite sufficiently for victory in the fall. As shown in Chapter 3, wide open scrambles for the nomination make it harder than ever to bring a party together in November, thereby giving the party with the least divisive nomination process a decided advantage. From the viewpoint of the 1980s, it is quite striking to note that Kennedy won in 1960 despite the fact that his party had the more divisive of the two nomination campaigns. Furthermore, the 1960 result was hardly a fluke in its day; Dwight Eisenhower won in 1952 despite a bitterly fought nomination race against Robert Taft.

The ideal path to victory in the candidate-centered age is a series of lopsided early primary wins, concessions from all the other candidates long before the convention, and a dull but harmonious convention that awards the second slot on the ticket to the leading opposition faction. Both Reagan in 1980 and Bush in 1988 followed this course, whereas their Democratic opponents suffered the consequences of long drawn-out internal fights. In neither case was the victor particularly popular (especially in Reagan's case), but united party support carried the day.

The decline of candidate popularity, as documented in Chapter 4, is one of the great ironies of the candidate-centered age. Whereas 65 percent of voters' comments about Kennedy and Nixon in 1960 were favorable, only 50 percent of the comments about Bush and Dukakis were positive in 1988. Perhaps it would have been better if voters had been more aware of the respective weaknesses later shown by both Nixon and Kennedy. But if a presidential election is to select a leader, is it not better to focus on who has the most leadership potential rather than which is the lesser of two evils?

With the greater scrutiny and internal opposition that candidates must now face, it is inevitable that they will end up publicly tainted in one way or another. In particular, no politician can endure opposition from a wide range of opponents in numerous contests without alienating a significant proportion of voters. Public competition also forces the candidates to take stands on controversial issues more than ever before. In every major state a candidate is forced into a corner on one issue or another (Democratic candidates in New York, for example, must state their position on whether the Israeli Embassy should be moved to Jerusalem). While voters may get a better sense of what the candidates will do in office, specific issue stands typically divide public opinion far more than the generalities that constituted the old brokered convention platforms.

Toward a Responsible Party Government?

In 1960 a frequently voiced concern among analysts of American elections was the lack of sufficient choice for the voting public. This was seen as symptomatic of the absence of "responsible party government." The electorate was faced with a choice between two centrists, and the most discussed issues of the 1960 campaign were Kennedy's Catholicism and youth, whether there was a missile gap (there wasn't), and what to do about the tiny islands of Quemoy and Matsu. Although subsequent history demonstrated profound policy differences between Kennedy and Nixon, few voters could have inferred them from the 1960 election campaign.

Starting with the Goldwater insurgency in 1964, voters were at times offered "a choice rather than a echo." Yet it was not until the 1980s that voters actually went for the choice rather than the echo. Reagan not only promised a markedly different course of action but was actually able to deliver on his major promises as well. Responsible party government advocates thus finally got the sort of decisiveness and action out of the electoral process that they had long desired.

Yet many of the worst fears of opponents of responsible party government were realized as well. These critics have generally preferred a more consensus-oriented, pluralistic model of democracy than was practiced during the elections of the 1980s. They have argued that given the diverse and multifaceted political culture in the United States, precipitous change should not occur because of a single choice between ideological polar opposites—as was the case in 1984 and 1988.

The idea of efficient majoritarian rule is indeed foreign to the American political system. As Robert Dahl has aptly pointed out, American government was founded primarily on the principle of protecting minorities rather than swiftly implementing majority desires.[4] The founders sought to make broad-based policy change difficult, even in cases where a popular mandate exists. They would thus find the survey data presented in this book concerning Reagan's policy mandate quite distressing. Chapter 5 shows there is little evidence to support claims of a mandate for more conservative government policies in 1980, aside from data on defense spending. Furthermore, in 1984 Reagan won a sweeping reelection victory *in spite* of his conservative stands rather than because of them. And in assessing the Reagan presidency in 1988, although people approved of economic prosperity at home and peace abroad, they continued to express lack of support for, or knowledge of, his policies.

Indeed, critics of the idea of responsible party government have long questioned whether the electorate is capable of the sort of ideological thought and action that the model requires. As Evron Kirkpatrick writes in his critique of the 1950 American Political Science Association (APSA) committee report on political parties,

> The cumulative impact of voting studies on the Committee model of the responsible party doctrine is, quite simply, devastating. Even if two programmatic but nondivisive parties were conceivable in the United States, the likelihood that their programs could be communicated to a mass electorate that would then choose in terms of the two alternatives structured by the parties, is inconceivable . . . *It is significant that neither side in the "responsible electorate" debate attributes to the electorate the information level about specific issues and policies required by the Committee model.*[5]

Given the argument presented here concerning the elections of the 1980s, an additional question to be considered is whether voters who are capable of employing policy criteria will choose to do so in the face of conflicting performance considerations.

With the decline of parties, attention has increasingly been focused on candidate-centered issues, which can be broadly categorized into either policy decisions (what the candidates will do or have done) or performance judgments (the results expected or produced). The former may polarize the electorate more than ever around candidate assessments, but the latter will take precedence in voting decisions. Thus we are left with the seeming paradox that although the 1980 election produced a profound ideological change in government policy it was not the result of strongly ideological voting. Unlike during previous presidential elections with an ideologically extreme candidate, such as 1964 and 1972, policy and performance considerations were at variance with each other for many voters. And as demonstrated in Chapter 6, given a choice between the two, performance evaluations clearly dominated the decision-making process.

It could of course be argued that the results of government actions have always taken precedence in voting behavior. The key difference in the candidate-centered age is that the likelihood of policy and performance factors pushing the electorate in opposite directions is far greater. In the past, policy and performance were tied together in the public's mind because of the central role of partisanship in political behavior. Some may have initially chosen their party on the basis of their upbringing, others on its performance during crucial periods of history, such as the Depression, and some no doubt on key long-term policy issues, such as civil rights. In any case, partisanship provided the psychological guidance necessary to interpret the political world in a consistent fashion. The sort of conflict between policy and performance evaluations experienced during the 1980s would not have occurred at a time when partisanship greatly influenced how people felt about both.

For this reason, such a conflict was probably inconceivable to members of the 1950 APSA committee that advocated a more responsible two-party system. It is therefore crucial to note that although proponents of responsible party government got the kind of programmatic choice and decisive action that they had always sought during the Reagan elections, it did not occur in the partisan-dominated environment they had envisioned. Thus the relatively clear choices offered the electorate in the Reagan elections cannot be judged as a fair test of the theory of responsible party government. This model can hardly work in an atmosphere where individual candidates dominate the political scene, where political parties have to struggle to maintain a modest degree of relevance, and where control of the presidency and Congress is regularly split between them.

By contrast, the Downsian model, as discussed in Chapter 1, fits the circumstances of the candidate-centered age much better than when it first appeared in the late 1950s. With the weakening of partisanship in recent years, both economic and sociological factors have become more important in shaping the presidential vote. In particular, it has been the economic performance variables that have been the major determinants of shifts in the vote. Whereas the prominence of short-term economic considerations has led recent elections to be decided on consensual performance factors, the increasing politicalization of group affiliations has fostered a more conflictual and polarized electoral process. Without a solid base of continuing partisan support, presidential candidate popularity has not surprisingly shown a long-term decline.

Perhaps the most amazing events of the 1980s occurred in 1981, when Reagan's major policy proposals were squarely dealt with. Looking back on the decade, we can see that decisive government action is the exception rather than the rule. As Stanley Cloud wrote in a late 1989 *Time* cover story, "Abroad and at home, more and more problems and opportunities are going unmet. Under the shadow of massive federal deficit that neither political party is willing to confront, a kind of neurosis of accepted limits has taken hold from one end of Pennsylvania Avenue to the other."[6]

As the candidate-centered age has progressed, politicians have learned to accept such limits as the normal order of things. Indeed, it is to their advantage to do so, as it enables

them to avoid being linked to others' agendas. L
incisively summarizes the current state of affairs a

> In our era of debilitated political parties, Washington is
> by 536 individual political entrepreneurs—one president, 100
> senators and 435 members of the House—each of whom got
> here essentially on his own. Each chooses the office he seeks,
> raises his own money, hires his own pollster and ad-maker
> and recruits his own volunteers.
>
> Each of them is scrambling to remain in office, no matter
> what. And each of them has commitments and objectives he
> considers paramount. When George Bush says, "Read my
> lips," each member of Congress replies, "I want mine."[7]

The result is that while government may or may not be the
problem, as Reagan argued, it definitely is no longer likely to
be the solution.

Notes

Introduction

1. See Martin P. Wattenberg, *The Decline of American Political Parties, 1952–1988* (Cambridge, Mass.: Harvard University Press, 1990), chap. 9.
2. Lester M. Salamon and Alan J. Abramson, "Governance: The Politics of Retrenchment," in John L. Palmer and Isabel V. Sawhill, eds., *The Reagan Record* (Cambridge, Mass.: Ballinger, 1984), p. 37.
3. Richard B. Wirthlin, "The Republican Strategy and Its Consequences," in Seymour Martin Lipset, ed., *Party Coalitions in the 1980s* (San Francisco: Institute for Contemporary Studies, 1981), p. 264.
4. Anthony Lewis, "The Tidal Wave," *New York Times*, November 6, 1980, p. A35.
5. For a summary of the papers and discussion at the 1981 American Political Science Association meeting see David S. Broder, "Election '80 Called Blip," *Washington Post*, September 5, 1981, p. A1; and Adam Clymer "Academics Debate Changes in Party Loyalty," *New York Times*, September 7, 1981, p. A7.
6. Stanley Kelley, *Interpreting Elections* (Princeton: Princeton University Press, 1983), p. 166.
7. Quoted in Ross K. Baker, "The Second Reagan Term," in Gerald Pomper (with colleagues), *The Election of 1984: Reports and Interpretations* (Chatham, N.J.: Chatham House, 1985), p. 134.
8. Doris Kearns, *Lyndon Johnson and the American Dream* (New York: Harper and Row, 1976), p. 216.
9. Quoted in David S. Broder, *The Party's Over: The Failure of Politics in America* (New York: Harper and Row, 1972), pp. 47–48.
10. See Bert A. Rockman, *The Leadership Question: The Presidency and the*

American Political System (New York: Praeger, 1984); and James David Barber, *The Presidential Character*, 3d ed. (Englewood Cliffs, N.J.: Prentice-Hall, 1985), chap. 15.

11. D. Lee Bawden and John L. Palmer, "Social Policy: Challenging the Welfare State," in Palmer and Sawhill, eds., *The Reagan Record*, p. 187.

12. John L. Palmer and Isabel V. Sawhill, "Overview," in Palmer and Sawhill, eds., *The Reagan Record*.

13. Ibid.

14. David S. Broder, "A Secure Place in History," *Washington Post Weekly*, February 4, 1985, p. 4.

15. Martin Shefter and Benjamin Ginsberg, "Why Reaganism Will Be with Us into the 21st Century," *Washington Post*, September 15, 1985, p. D4.

16. Walter Dean Burnham, *The Current Crisis in American Politics* (New York: Oxford University Press, 1982), p. 10.

17. V. O. Key, Jr., *The Responsible Electorate: Rationality in Presidential Voting, 1936–1960* (New York: Random House, 1966), p. 61.

18. Ibid.

19. Quoted in William Schneider, "Incumbency Saved the Democrats This Time, But What about the Next?" *Los Angeles Times*, November 11, 1984, part 5, pp. 1 and 3.

20. Quoted in Barry Sussman, "His Approval Rating and 50 Cents Will Get Reagan a Cup of Coffee," *Washington Post Weekly*, September 23, 1985 p. 37.

21. The term "double retrospective election" was coined by Herbert F. Weisberg in "The Electoral Kaleidoscope: Political Change in the Polarizing Election of 1984," p. 7. Paper presented at the annual meeting of the American Political Science Association, 1985.

22. See Paul R. Abramson, John H. Aldrich, and David W. Rohde, *Change and Continuity in the 1988 Elections* (Washington, D.C.: Congressional Quarterly, 1990).

1. Theories of Voting

1. Jean M. Converse, *Survey Research in the United States: Roots and Emergence, 1890–1960* (Berkeley: University of California Press, 1987), pp. 402–403.

2. Paul F. Lazarsfeld, Bernard R. Berelson, and Hazel Gaudet, *The People's Choice* (New York: Columbia University Press, 1944).

3. Bernard R. Berelson, Paul F. Lazarsfeld, and William N. McPhee, *Voting: A Study of Opinion Formation in a Presidential Campaign* (Chicago: University of Chicago Press, 1954).

4. Ibid., p. 301.

5. Ibid., p. 316.

6. Angus Campbell, Gerald Gurin, and Warren E. Miller, *The Voter Decides* (Evanston, Ill.: Row, Peterson, and Co., 1954).

7. Ibid., p. 85.

8. Angus Campbell, Philip E. Converse, Warren E. Miller, and Donald E. Stokes, *The American Voter* (New York: Wiley, 1960).

9. Ibid., p. 9.

10. Ibid., p. 36.

11. Anthony Downs, *An Economic Theory of Democracy* (New York: Harper and Row, 1957).

12. Ibid., chap. 12.

13. Ibid., p. 36.

14. Ibid., p. 40.

15. Ibid., p. x.

16. The journals considered as political science are: *American Political Science Review, American Journal of Political Science, Journal of Politics, Western Political Quarterly, European Journal of Political Research, Canadian Journal of Political Science, British Journal of Political Science, Polity, PS: Political Science and Politics, Legislative Studies Quarterly, Comparative Political Studies, Comparative Politics, Political Studies,* and *Political Science Quarterly.*

17. Key, *The Responsible Electorate*, p. 2.

18. Downs, *An Economic Theory*, p. 137.

19. Ibid., p. 139.

20. See James I. Lengle, *Representation and Presidential Primaries: The Democratic Party in the Post-Reform Era* (Westport, Conn.: Greenwood Press, 1981).

21. Byron E. Shafer, *Bifurcated Politics: Evolution and Reform in the National Party Convention* (Cambridge, Mass.: Harvard University Press, 1988).

22. Campbell et al., *The American Voter*, pp. 549–550.

23. Downs, *An Economic Theory*, p. 98.

24. Donald E. Stokes, "Spatial Models of Party Competition," in Angus Campbell et al., *Elections and the Political Order* (New York: Wiley, 1966), p. 170.

25. Downs, *An Economic Theory*, p. 44.

26. The problem of equal weighting of responses is addressed at length in Kelley, *Interpreting Elections*, Appendix 1. Although Kelley finds statistical evidence for the application of differential weights, his conclusion is that "the constraining assumption of the equal weighting of issues makes no difference in one's ability to account for votes."

27. Downs, *An Economic Theory*, p. 116.

28. The economic codes for 1952 to 1968 are as follows: 80–81, 420–460, 490–493, 541–560. For 1972 to 1984 the comparable codes are: 605–606, 805–808, 811–812, 829–831, 837–838, 901–945, 952–961, 965–967, 1001–1003, 1007–1009, 1025–1027.

29. The partisan codes from 1952 to 1968 are 800–820 and 700–711. For 1972 to 1984 the comparable codes are as follows: 53–54, 101–122, 133–134, 500–503, 1202–1206.

30. From 1952 to 1968 the sociological codes are as follows: 251–253, 260–263, 391, 712–790. After 1968 the comparable codes are: 425–426, 455–456, 1207–1297.

31. See Campbell et al., *The American Voter*, pp. 45–48.

32. Ibid., p. 139.

33. See Robert Huckfeldt and John Sprague, "Networks in Context: The Social Flow of Political Information," *American Political Science Review* 81 (1987): 1197–1216; and John Books and Charles Prysby, "Studying Contextual Effects on Political Behavior: A Research Inventory and Agenda," *American Politics Quarterly* 16 (1988): 211–238.

2. Dealignment in the Electorate

1. Ronald Inglehart and Avram Hochstein, "Alignment and Dealignment of the Electorate in France and the United States," *Comparative Political Studies* 5 (1972): 343–372.

2. Walter Dean Burnham, *Critical Elections and the Mainsprings of American Politics* (New York: Norton, 1970).

3. Walter Dean Burnham, "The 1984 Elections and the Future of American Politics," in Ellis Sandoz and Cecil V. Crabb, Jr., eds., *Election 84: Landslide without a Mandate?* (New York: Mentor, 1985), p. 248.

4. Quoted in Austin Ranney, *Curing the Mischiefs of Faction: Party Reform in America* (Berkeley: University of California Press, 1975), p. 125.

5. Quoted in Leon D. Epstein, *Political Parties in the American Mold* (Madison, Wis.: University of Wisconsin Press, 1986), p. 5.

6. Jack Dennis, "Trends in Public Support for the American Party System," *British Journal of Political Science* 5 (1975): 187–230.
7. Larry J. Sabato, *The Party's Just Begun: Shaping Political Parties for America's Future* (Glenview, Ill.: Scott, Foresman and Co., 1988), p. 133.
8. Paul Allen Beck, "The Dealignment Era in America," in Russell J. Dalton et. al., eds., *Electoral Change in Advanced Industrial Democracies: Realignment or Dealignment?* (Princeton: Princeton University Press, 1984).
9. Burnham, "The 1984 Elections," p. 235.
10. See Wattenberg, *The Decline of American Political Parties*, p. 140.
11. Bruce Keith et al., "The Myth of the Independent Voter." Paper presented at the annual meeting of the American Political Science Association, 1977.
12. Ibid., p. 3.
13. Sabato, *The Party's Just Begun*, p. 117.
14. Norman H. Nie, Sidney Verba, and John R. Petrocik, *The Changing American Voter* (Cambridge, Mass.: Harvard University Press, 1976).
15. Philip E. Converse, "The Nature of Belief Systems in Mass Publics," in David E. Apter, ed., *Ideology and Discontent* (Glencoe, Ill.: Free Press, 1964).
16. See Philip E. Converse and Gregory B. Markus, "Plus ça change . . . The New CPS Election Study Panel," *American Political Science Review* 73 (1979): 32–49; and M. Kent Jennings and Gregory B. Markus, "Partisan Orientations over the Long Haul: Results from the Three-Wave Political Socialization Study," *American Political Science Review* 78 (1984): 1000–1018.
17. Epstein, *Political Parties in the American Mold*, p. 246.
18. Ibid., p. 346.
19. Russell J. Dalton, Scott C. Flanagan, and Paul Allen Beck, "Political Forces and Partisan Change," in Dalton et al., eds., *Electoral Change*, p. 462.

3. The Era of Party Disunity

1. Emmett H. Buell, Jr., "Divisive Primaries and Participation in Fall Presidential Campaigns: A Study of 1984 New Hampshire Primary Activists," *American Politics Quarterly* 14 (1986): 376–390.
2. Walter J. Stone, "Prenomination Candidate Choice and General

Election Behavior: Iowa Presidential Activists in 1980," *American Journal of Political Science* 28 (1984): 361–378.

3. James I. Lengle, "Divisive Presidential Primaries and Party Electoral Prospects, 1932–1976," *American Politics Quarterly* 8 (1980): 261–277.

4. Patrick J. Kenney and Tom W. Rice, "The Relationship between Divisive Primaries and General Election Outcomes," *American Journal of Political Science* 31 (1987): 31–44.

5. "The Democrats: Caucus Fatigue," *Newsweek*, April 2, 1984, p. 30.

6. J. Morgan Kousser, *The Shaping of Southern Politics: Suffrage Restriction and the Establishment of the One-Party South, 1880–1910* (New Haven: Yale University Press, 1974), p. 80.

7. Russell Baker, "Stevenson, Kefauver Find Agreement in TV Debate," *New York Times*, May 22, 1956, p. 1.

8. "Humphrey Denies League against JFK in Debate by 2 Senators," *Los Angeles Times*, May 5, 1960, p. 1.

9. "GOP Attacks 'Debate,' Demands Equal Time," *Washington Post*, May 6, 1960, p. 2.

10. Howell Raines, "Democrats' Forum Becomes a Vehicle to Criticize Hart," *New York Times*, March 12, 1984, pp. Al and B9.

11. Nelson W. Polsby, *Consequences of Party Reform* (New York: Oxford University Press, 1983), pp. 149, 256.

12. "Cut Out the Rough Stuff," *Time*, March 23, 1987, p. 29.

13. Bob Drogin and Thomas B. Rosenstiel, "Dukakis, Jackson Face Task of Forging Alliance in Party," *Los Angeles Times*, May 16, 1988, p. 14.

14. David R. Runkel, ed., *Campaign for President: The Managers Look at '88* (Dover, Mass.: Auburn, 1989), p. 104.

15. Larry M. Bartels, *Presidential Primaries and the Dynamics of Public Choice* (Princeton: Princeton University Press, 1988), p. 287.

16. See Shafer, *Bifurcated Politics*.

17. Nelson W. Polsby and Aaron Wildavsky, *Presidential Elections*, 7th ed. (New York: Free Press, 1988), pp. 155–156.

18. Runkel, *Campaign for President*, p. 230.

4. Presidential Popularity in Decline

1. For a useful summary see George C. Edwards and Stephen J. Wayne, *Presidential Leadership: Politics and Policy Making* (New York: St. Martin's Press, 1985), chap. 4.

2. See John E. Mueller, *War, Presidents, and Public Opinion* (New York: Wiley, 1973); and James A. Stimson, "Public Support for American Presidents: A Cycle Model," *Public Opinion Quarterly* 40 (1976): 1–21.

3. See Richard A. Brody, "International Crises: A Rallying Point for the President?" *Public Opinion*, December / January 1984, 41–43; and Kristen R. Monroe, *Presidential Popularity and the Economy* (New York: Praeger, 1984).

4. Robert Dallek, *Ronald Reagan: The Politics of Symbolism* (Cambridge, Mass.: Harvard University Press, 1984), p. 3.

5. Elliot King and Michael Schudson, "The Press and the Illusion of Public Opinion: The Strange Case of Ronald Reagan's 'Popularity,' " forthcoming in Theodore Glaser and Charles Salmon, eds. *Public Opinion and the Communication of Consent* (New York: Guilford, 1991).

6. Ibid., pp. 18–19.

7. See, for example, Michael Baruch Grossman and Martha Joynt Kumar, *Portraying the President: The White House and the News Media* (Baltimore: Johns Hopkins University Press, 1981), chap. 11.

8. James David Barber, *The Presidential Character: Predicting Performance in the White House*, 3d ed. (Englewood Cliffs, N.J.: Prentice-Hall, 1985), p. 469.

9. See George C. Edwards III, "Comparing Chief Executives," *Public Opinion*, June / July 1985, 51.

10. Gallup presidential approval ratings by party can be found for each year from 1953 to 1988 in George C. Edwards III, with Alec Gallup, *Presidential Approval: A Sourcebook* (Baltimore: Johns Hopkins University Press, 1990), chap. 1. For Reagan's second term the average difference in approval ratings between Democratic and Republican identifiers was 51 percent.

11. The data on Senate and House candidates are from the 1988 NES Senate Study conducted by phone. Because a roughly equal number of people were interviewed in each state, the sample must be weighted in order to be representative of the nation as a whole. I have used the number of congressional districts per state as the weighting factor. Substantively, the results were only slightly changed by weighting the data in this fashion.

12. See Wattenberg, *The Decline of American Political Parties*.

13. These data are part of a research project on candidate evaluations done in conjuction with Arthur Miller and Oksana Malanchuk. See

Arthur H. Miller, Martin P. Wattenberg, and Oksana Malanchuk, "Schematic Assessments of Presidential Candidates," *American Political Science Review* 80 (1986): 521–540. The appendix to this article includes the exact codes assigned to each of the five dimensions of personal attributes.

14. Thomas E. Cronin, "The Presidential Election of 1984." In Sandoz and Crabb, eds., *Election 84*, p. 36.

5. Was There a Mandate?

1. For several insightful reviews of this literature see Herbert B. Asher, *Presidential Elections and American Politics*, 4th ed. (Homewood, Ill.: Dorsey, 1988), chap. 4; Philip E. Converse, "Public Opinion and Voting Behavior," in Fred I. Greenstein and Nelson W. Polsby, eds., *Handbook of Political Science*, vol. 4. (Reading, Mass.: Addison-Wesley, 1975); and John H. Kessel, "The Issues in Issue Voting," *American Political Science Review* 66 (1972): 459–465.

2. Donald E. Stokes, "Spatial Models of Party Competition," in Angus Campbell, Philip E. Converse, Warren E. Miller, and Donald E. Stokes, *Elections and the Political Order* (New York: Wiley, 1966).

3. E. E. Schattschneider, *The Semi-Sovereign People: A Realist's View of Democracy in America* (Hinsdale, Ill.: Dryden Press, 1960).

4. J. Merrill Shanks and Warren E. Miller, "Policy Direction and Performance Evaluation: Complementary Explanations of the Reagan Elections." Paper presented at the annual meeting of the American Political Science Association, 1985.

5. Charles H. Franklin, "Policy, Performance, and the Adjustment of Issue Preferences." Paper presented at the annual meeting of the Midwest Political Science Association, 1985.

6. King and Schudson, "The Press and the Illusion of Public Opinion."

7. Samuel Popkin, "The Donkey's Dilemma: White Men Don't Vote Democratic," *Washington Post*, November 11, 1984, p. D1.

8. See Pamela Johnston Conover and Stanley Feldman, "The Origins and Meanings of Liberal/Conservative Identifications," *American Journal of Political Science* 25 (1981): 617–645; and Teresa E. Levitan and Warren E. Miller, "Ideological Interpretations of Presidential Elections," *American Political Science Review* 76 (1979): 751–771.

9. See Richard Scammon and Ben J. Wattenberg, *The Real Majority*

(New York: Berkley Publishing Co., 1970); and Warren E. Miller and Teresa E. Levitan, *Leadership and Change: The New Politics and the American Electorate* (Cambridge, Mass.: Winthrop Publishers, 1976).

10. Tom W. Smith, "That Which We Call Welfare by Any Other Name Would Smell Sweeter: An Analysis of the Impact of Question Wording on Response Patterns," *Public Opinion Quarterly* 51 (1987): 75–83.

11. See Richard A. Brody and Benjamin I. Page, "Comment: The Assessment of Policy Voting," *American Political Science Review* 66 (1972): 450–458; and Gregory B. Markus and Philip E. Converse, "A Dynamic Simultaneous Equation Model of Electoral Choice," *American Political Science Review* 73 (1979): 1050–1070.

12. Shanks and Miller, "Policy Direction and Performance Evaluation," p. 35.

13. By actually reading the interview protocols, Arthur Miller and I were able to determine more precisely whether the responses were predominately policy or performance oriented. Our coding, however, was done on the basis of the entire answer to each question rather than each individual response, and therefore cannot be used to pinpoint specific areas of policy debate. For the results of this study, see Arthur H. Miller and Martin P. Wattenberg, "Throwing the Rascals Out: Policy and Performance Voting in Presidential Elections, 1952–1980," *American Political Science Review* 79 (1985): 359–372.

14. For the period from 1952 to 1980, 58.7 percent of candidate attribute comments were positive compared to 54.2 percent for performance and 48.5 percent for policy responses. See Miller and Wattenberg, ibid., p. 364.

15. Quoted in Stanley Kelley, *Interpreting Elections*, pp. 3–4.

6. Performance-Based Voting

1. See Wattenberg, *The Decline of American Political Parties*, chaps. 5, 8, and 9.

2. See Philip E. Converse, "The Nature of Belief Systems in Mass Publics," in Apter, ed., *Ideology and Discontent*.

3. John Zaller, "Toward a Theory of the Survey Response," p. 3. Paper presented at the annual meeting of the American Political Science Association, 1984.

4. See Samuel Popkin et al., "Comment: What Have You Done for Me Lately? Toward an Investment Theory of Voting," *American Political Science Review* 70 (1976): 779–805.

5. Morris P. Fiorina, *Retrospective Voting in American National Elections* (New Haven: Yale University Press, 1981), chap. 2.

6. Campbell et al., *The American Voter*, p. 259, emphasis added.

7. Ibid.

8. Ibid., p. 260.

9. Ibid.

10. Fiorina, *Retrospective Voting*, p. 5.

11. Benjamin I. Page, *Choices and Echos in Presidential Elections: Rational Man and Electoral Democracy* (Chicago: University of Chicago Press, 1978), p. 222.

12. Key, *The Responsible Electorate*, p. 76.

13. Richard A. Brody and Lee Sigelman, "Presidential Popularity and Presidential Elections: An Update and Extension," *Public Opinion Quarterly* 47 (1983): 325–328.

14. D. Roderick Kiewiet and Douglas Rivers, "The Economic Basis of Reagan's Appeal," in John E. Chubb and Paul E. Peterson, eds., *The New Direction in American Politics* (Washington, D.C.: Brookings, 1985), p. 87.

15. Warren E. Miller and J. Merrill Shanks, "Policy Directions and Presidential Leadership: Alternative Interpretations of the 1980 Presidential Election. Paper presented at the annual meeting of the American Political Science Association, 1981; and Shanks and Miller, "Policy Direction and Performance Evaluation."

16. Campbell et al., *The American Voter*, chap. 2.

17. Shanks and Miller, "Policy Direction and Performance Evaluation," p. 6.

18. See Fiorina, *Retrospective Voting*.

19. See D. Roderick Kiewiet, *Microeconomics and Macropolitics: The Electoral Effects of Economic Issues* (Chicago: University of Chicago Press, 1983).

20. Curtis B. Gans, "Apathy Stands In as American Condition," *Los Angeles Times*, March 12, 1986, part 2, p. 13.

21. Samuel Kernell, "Presidential Popularity and Negative Voting: An Alternative Explanation of the Midterm Congressional Decline of the President's Party," *American Political Science Review* (1977): 51.

22. Ibid., p. 53.

23. The wording of the question in the *New York Times* / CBS poll was as follows: "Did you decide on your candidate mainly because you liked him, or because you didn't like the others?" Positive voters outnumbered negative voters by margins of 73 to 27 in 1976, 56 to 44 in 1980, and 57 to 43 in 1988.

24. It is also of interest to note that the number of positive comments concerning the presidential candidates has consistently had a higher correlation with turnout than the number of negative comments has.

25. These results are largely safe from multicollinearity problems because of the relatively weak relationship between the number of positive and negative comments about the candidates. For example, in 1964 this correlation was $-.31$ for Johnson and $-.23$ for Goldwater. In 1984 the comparable figures were $-.14$ for Mondale and $-.13$ for Reagan. The lack of a strong negative correlation adds further methodological validity to this technique of separating positive from negative attitudes, as it demonstrates that the two tap distinctly different dimensions of feelings.

26. The policy questions included the following items: government-guaranteed jobs, government spending, size of the federal government, inflation-unemployment tradeoff (1980 only), defense spending, detente with Soviet Union, Central America involvement (1984 only), aid to minorities, pace of the civil rights movement, busing (1980 and 1984 only), preferential treatment for women seeking jobs, Equal Rights Amendment (1980 only), role of women in society, abortion, and school prayer. Each variable was trichotomized into liberal, conservative, and moderate/don't know responses, with the index being formed by subtracting the number of liberal responses from the number of conservative ones.

7. The Impact of Candidate-Centered Politics

1. See Anthony King, ed., *The New American Political System*, 2d ed. (Washington, D.C.: American Enterprise Institute, 1990).

2. Charles Brereton, *First in the Nation: New Hampshire and the Premier Presidential Primary* (Portsmouth, N.H.: Peter E. Randall, 1987).

3. Theodore H. White, *The Making of the President, 1960* (New York: Atheneum, 1961), p. 87.

4. Robert Dahl, *A Preface to Democratic Theory* (Chicago: University of Chicago Press, 1956).

5. Evron Kirkpatrick, "Toward a More Responsible Party System: Political Science, Policy Science, or Pseudo-Science?" in Jeff Fishel, ed., *Parties and Elections in an Anti-Party Age* (Bloomington: Indiana University Press, 1978), pp. 40–41.

6. Stanley W. Cloud, "The Can't Do Government," *Time*, October 23, 1989, p. 29.

7. David S. Broder, "Gutless Government," *Washington Post Weekly*, November 6, 1989, p. 4.

Index

Abortion, 70, 103, 105, 117, 118, 119, 121, 123
Abramson, Alan, 4
Abstention, 17
Affirmative action, 70, 105, 106
Afghanistan, 109, 114, 142
Age, of candidates, 82, 84, 160
Alabama, 50, 51
Alienation hypothesis, 41–42
American Political Science Association (APSA), 162, 163
American Social Attitudes Data Sourcebook, 1947–1978 (Converse et al.), 108
American Voter, The (Campbell et al.), 11, 15, 17, 18, 19, 20, 24, 132–133, 141
Anderson, John, 4, 53, 76, 100
Appearance, of candidates, 81, 82, 85
Approval ratings, 67, 70, 132, 134–155. *See also* Performance-centered voting
Arkansas, 50, 51, 56
Arms control, 139
Atlanta, 55
Attitudes, voters', 130–131, 142
Atwater, Lee, 56
Australian ballot, 33

Background, of candidates, 82, 84

Bagehot, Walter, 58
Baker, Howard, 23
Baker, James, 9
Ballot reform, 33
Barber, James David, 70
Beck, Paul Allen, 34, 45
Berelson, Bernard R., 14, 15, 19
Bifurcated Politics (Shafer), 57
Bitburg, West Germany, 69
Blacks, 106–108, 112–113, 143. *See also* Minority aid
Britain, 58
Broder, David S., 7, 165
Brody, Richard A., 135
Bryan, William Jennings, 2, 11
Budget, 6, 8, 68, 70, 93, 109, 137, 138, 140, 146, 147, 164. *See also* Military spending; Social services spending; Spending
Buell, Emmett, 49
Burnham, Walter Dean, 7, 31, 32, 36, 37
Bush, George, 3, 9, 10, 11, 38, 50, 51, 52, 53, 54, 56, 60, 65, 66, 67, 69, 72, 75, 76, 79, 80, 83, 85, 87, 88, 89, 90, 97, 101, 112–113, 116, 122, 123, 125, 128, 151, 152, 158, 159, 160, 165
Busing, 103, 105

California, 52, 53, 56, 68
Campaign managers, 60
Campbell, Angus, 11, 19, 24, 28, 132–133
Candidate-centered voting, 1, 2, 11–12, 39, 52, 73, 156–165
Candidate policy proximities, 110–123
Candidate popularity. *See* Popularity
Carter, Jimmy, 3, 4, 8, 10, 11, 41, 52, 53, 60, 63, 67, 73, 76, 78, 79, 83, 84, 85, 86, 88, 89, 94, 99–100, 101, 109, 111, 112, 114–115, 116, 117, 129, 134, 135, 136, 137, 138, 142, 148, 151, 152, 153, 154–155
Carter administration, 6, 10, 28
Caucus fatigue, 54
Caucus voters, 22
CBS (Columbia Broadcasting System), 58. *See also New York Times*/CBS exit polls
Cementing elections, 10
Census data, 13–14
Central American involvement, 70, 101, 112, 144, 145
Charisma, of candidates, 81, 82, 85, 86, 89
Cheney, Richard, 9
Chicago, 158
China, 126, 141
Church, and relation to state, 119
Citation analysis, 17–20
Civil rights, 91, 102–103, 105–106, 163
Civil service, 33
Cloud, Stanley, 164
Columbia University, Bureau of Applied Social Research, 14
Committee for the Study of the Electorate, 148
Communication skills, 68–69
Communism, 126
Competence, of candidates, 81, 82, 84, 85, 139
Conceptualization levels, 43

Congress, 5, 6, 7, 9, 10, 37–38, 125, 164, 165
Congressional elections, 1–2, 36–39, 46, 79–80, 149
Congressional party delegations, 23
Congressional Quarterly, 52
Conservatism, 95–97, 114, 118, 119, 121, 126, 128, 161
Contras. *See* Iran/Contra scandal
Conventions, 46, 47–48, 56–60, 63, 65, 160
Converse, Philip, 43, 108
Coolidge, Calvin, 48
Corrigan, John, 60
Corruption, 33
Crabb, Cecil V., Jr., 37
Crime, 108, 121, 122–123
Critical Elections and the Mainsprings of American Politics (Burnham), 31
Cronin, Thomas, 89

Dahl, Robert, 161
Dalleck, Robert, 67
Dalton, Russell J., 45
Dealignment of electorate, 12, 28, 30, 31–46
Death penalty, 121, 123
Debates, 54–55
Debt. *See* Budget
Defense spending. *See* Military spending
Democratic convention. *See* Conventions
Democratic Party, 42, 55. *See also* Democrats; Parties
Democrats, 2, 9, 11, 23, 33, 36, 39–45, 47–48, 49, 50, 54, 55–56, 58, 59–60, 63–64, 65, 78–79, 99, 104, 115, 125, 149–150, 160
Depression, 133, 163
Des Moines, 158
Detente, 119, 126, 127, 139, 141, 144
Direct mail, 28

Dolan, Terry, 95
Dole, Robert, 46, 50, 59, 158
Domestic spending. *See* Spending
Double retrospective elections, 10
Downs, Anthony, 15–16, 18, 19, 20, 21, 22, 23–25, 26, 29, 164
Du Pont, Pierre S., 158
Dukakis, Michael, 50, 51, 52, 56, 59, 60, 79, 83, 87, 88, 89, 90, 97, 112–113, 116, 122–123, 148, 152, 157, 158, 160

Echo chamber theory, 20–21
Economic inequality, 106
Economic theories, 15–16, 21–25, 26–28, 29, 164
Economic Theory of Democracy, An (Downs), 17, 18–20, 21, 24
Economy, 132, 134, 135, 136, 137–138, 140, 141, 144, 145, 146, 147, 152–153, 154, 155, 162
Education, 108, 119, 121, 124, 125–126, 127, 128, 147
Edwards, George, 78
Eisenhower, Dwight D., 24, 28, 46, 48, 73, 75, 76, 77, 78, 79, 82, 83, 84, 85, 90–91, 159
Eisenhower era, 43
Elderly aid, 120
Election '84 (Sandoz and Crabb), 37
Environment, 108, 124, 125–126, 128, 147
Epstein, Leon, 45
Equal Rights Amendment, 105, 117, 118
Equal time, 55
Exit poll data, 50–51, 149

Falwell, Jerry, 95
Favorability ratings, 50–51
Favorite son candidate, 49
Feeling thermometer ratings, 64, 80, 96, 98, 99, 148

Ferraro, Geraldine, 59
Fiorina, Morris, 132, 133
Fischer, Paul, 158
Flanagan, Scott C., 45
Floating voters, 43
Florida, 51, 54
Ford, Gerald, 52, 56, 59, 60, 78, 83, 85, 101
Foreign aid, 108, 109, 127
Foreign policy, 118, 127, 134, 135, 136, 140, 141, 142, 144, 146, 153, 155
Founding Fathers, 32, 161
France, 31
Franklin, Charles, 94
Funnel of causality concept, 141

Gallup poll, 34, 35, 67, 71, 78, 132
Gans, Curtis, 148
Gaudet, Hazel, 14
General Social Surveys, 108
Georgia, 51
Ginsberg, Benjamin, 7
Goldwater, Barry, 8, 52, 53, 59, 60, 65, 73, 82, 83, 95, 148, 149, 150, 161
Gore, Albert, 23, 56
Government power, 102–104, 119, 165
Government services, 112–113, 114, 116, 118, 119
Great communicator image, 68–69
Great Society, 109
Gross national product, 7
Gubernatorial votes, 36
Gun control, 121, 123

Haig, Alexander, 158
Harris poll, 70
Hart, Gary, 56, 59, 63, 115
Health insurance, 102–103, 106, 112–113, 121
Hochstein, Avram, 31
Hoover, Herbert, 6, 11, 133

Horton, Willie, 56, 122, 148
House candidates, 79–80
House Rebublican Policy Commit-
tee, 9
Humphrey, Hubert, 54–55, 60, 63, 83,
87, 104

Idaho, 56
Ideology, 22–24, 49, 59, 65, 95–101,
107, 118, 119, 126, 128, 161, 162–
163
Illinois, 51, 53
Incumbency, 1–2, 53, 76–77, 83, 93–
94
Independents, 40, 41, 44, 65
Inflation, 5, 135, 137, 138, 139, 143
Inglehart, Ronald, 31
Integrity, of candidates, 81–84, 85, 89
Interest groups, 28, 59
Interest rates, 143
Interpreting Elections (Kelley), 5
Iowa, 49, 157–158
Iran/Contra scandal, 69, 86, 89, 90,
121, 127, 128, 139
Iranian hostage crisis, 5, 109–110,
135, 136, 137, 142
Israeli Embassy, 160

Jackson, Henry, 55
Jackson, Jesse, 59–60, 115
Jennings-Niemi Socialization Study,
34, 35
Jerusalem, 160
Johnson, Lyndon B., 5, 60, 73, 77, 83,
86, 105, 148, 149
Jobs programs, 102–103, 106, 112–
113, 116, 141, 144, 145, 146
Journalism. *See* Mass media

Kefauver, Estes, 54, 157
Keith, Bruce, 40
Kelley, Stanley, 5, 18–20
Kemp, Jack, 158
Kennedy, Edward, 63

Kennedy, John F., 48, 54–55, 56, 73,
76, 79, 83, 84, 115, 149, 156, 157,
158, 159, 160, 161
Kennedy era, 43
Kenney, Patrick, 49, 50
Kernell, Samuel, 148–149
Key, V. O., Jr., 8, 9, 20–21, 134
Kiewiet, D. Roderick, 139
King, Anthony, 156
King, Elliot, 68
Kirk, Paul, 55
Kirkpatrick, Evron, 162
Korea, 91
Kousser, J. Morgan, 54

LaFollette, Robert, 33
Landon, Alf, 11
Lazarsfeld, Paul, 14
Leadership, 3, 160
Lebanon, 69
Lewis, Anthony, 4
Liberalism, 97, 114, 115, 120, 121, 123,
126, 128
Lincoln, Abraham, 2
Lippmann, Walter, 128
Louisiana, 51

Making of the President, The (White), 158
Mandate. *See* Policy voting
Massachusetts, 51, 156
Mass media, 4, 21, 39, 54, 57, 68, 85,
90, 131. *See also* Television
Matsu, 160
McGovern, George, 52, 53, 60, 73, 82,
83, 95, 100, 148, 150
Merit criteria for jobs, 33
Michel, Bob, 46
Military spending, 5, 6, 108, 109–110,
111, 112–113, 114, 115, 117, 118,
119, 120, 121, 122, 123, 124, 125,
126–127, 128–129, 136, 141, 142,
143, 144, 145, 146, 147, 161
Miller, Warren E., 94, 111, 141, 142,
144

Miller, William, 59
Minnesota, 67
Minority aid, 102–103, 106, 108, 112–113, 153
Minority protection, 161
Missile gap, 160
Mississippi, 50, 51
Missouri, 50, 51
Monarchy, 58
Mondale, Walter, 10, 11, 28, 29, 45, 49, 52, 53, 55, 56, 60, 63, 64, 67, 68, 75, 77, 83, 87, 88, 104, 115, 117, 120, 123, 138, 148, 152, 153
Montana, 56
Mozambique, 56

National Election Studies, 3, 25–29, 43–44, 67, 70–91, 96–129, 132
    1952: 42, 72–75, 76, 150
    1956: 42, 72–75, 77, 78, 150
    1960: 43, 72–73, 74, 76, 149, 150
    1964: 62, 72–73, 74, 77, 97, 149, 150
    1968: 42, 62, 72, 74, 76, 132, 150
    1972: 62, 72, 73, 74, 77, 96, 98, 100, 101, 150
    1976: 62, 72, 74, 76, 100, 101, 150
    1980: 35, 40, 62, 72, 73–75, 76, 78, 87, 88, 111–115, 116, 117, 118, 122, 134–137, 138–139, 150, 151, 152, 153
    1984: 27–28, 42, 43, 44, 62, 71, 72, 73–75, 77–78, 79, 80, 88, 100, 111–114, 115, 116, 117, 119–120, 122, 134–139, 144–146, 150, 151, 152, 153
    1988: 42, 62, 72, 74, 76, 79, 80, 88, 98, 111–113, 116, 117, 121, 122–129, 134–136, 139–140, 146–147, 150, 152
National security, 146, 147
"Nature of the times" voting, 132, 133
NBC (National Broadcasting System), 58
Negative campaigning, 123

Negative momentum, 56
Negative voting, 148–155
Nevada, 56
New Deal, 7, 9, 95, 143, 159
New Hampshire, 49, 52, 53, 158
Newsweek, 53
New York, 33, 51, 56, 158, 160
New York Times, 4, 35, 54, 55
New York Times/CBS exit polls, 51, 149
Nie, Norman, 41
Nixon, Richard M., 60, 73, 76, 77, 79, 83, 84, 86, 87, 100, 101, 104, 109, 126, 148, 158, 159, 160
Nomination fighting index, 60–62
Nomination margin, 52–53
Nomination process, 23, 33, 47–65, 157–158, 159. *See also* Primaries
Noncentrist candidates and positions, 22, 23
North Carolina, 51
Nuclear freeze, 119, 122
Nunn, Sam, 23

Oil prices, 154
Oklahoma, 50, 51
O'Neill, Tip, 5, 68
Open-ended data, 26, 67, 70, 79, 87, 116–129, 132, 136–140
Oregon, 52

Page, Benjamin, 133
Parties, 1, 2, 33–46, 64, 131, 134, 149–150, 155, 158, 163–164, 165
Partisan images, 43–46
Partisanship, 2, 12, 15, 22, 26, 27, 28, 29, 30, 31–65, 73, 75, 158, 159
Party bosses, 33
Party discipline, 55–56
Peace, 137, 138, 139, 140, 144, 145, 162
People's Choice, The (Lazarsfeld et al.), 14
Performance-centered voting, 4, 12,

Performance-centered voting (*con't.*)
92–95, 130–155, 163; summary
measure of, 152–153
Personal attributes, 80–91, 139
Petrocik, John, 41
Phantom Public, The (Lippmann), 128
Polarization, 3
Policy change, 3, 7–11, 12, 101–129
Policy voting, 92–129; compared with
performance voting, 130–155, 160–
163; summary measure of, 152–153
Political ignorance, 43
Political parties. *See* Parties
Political science journals, 20
Polls, 34, 35, 50–51, 66–67, 70, 71, 78,
96, 130–131, 149
Pollution, 121, 127
Polsby, Nelson, 55, 59
Popkin, Samuel, 96
Popularity, 12, 50–51, 63, 65, 66–91,
159–160
Popular press. *See* Mass media
Popular vote, 52, 67
Popular will, 128
Poverty aid, 108, 109, 124, 143, 147
Presidential elections, 36, 48
    1896: 10, 11
    1900: 10, 11
    1912: 47
    1924: 47–48
    1932: 10, 28
    1936: 10, 11
    1940: 14
    1948: 15, 48
    1952: 15, 48, 157
    1956: 34, 53, 57, 78
    1960: 48, 57, 73, 87, 156–161, 162–
    163
    1964: 52, 57, 60, 73, 81–82, 95, 148,
    161, 163
    1968: 57, 60, 63, 86, 87, 104, 148
    1972: 52, 57, 60, 73, 95, 104, 142,
    148, 163
    1976: 52, 53, 55, 57, 60, 84, 104, 148

    1980: 52, 53, 55, 57, 60, 63, 67, 68,
    73, 77, 82, 84, 85, 93, 95, 100, 110,
    111–115, 116, 117–118, 122, 134–
    137, 138, 139, 142, 148, 151, 153,
    161, 162–163
    1984: 11, 27–28, 29, 38, 49, 52, 53,
    55, 57, 60, 63–64, 71, 73, 75, 77–78,
    79, 80, 82, 85, 86, 89, 111–114, 115,
    116, 117, 118, 119–120, 122, 134–
    139, 144–146, 148, 151, 154–155, 161
    1988: 11, 23, 38, 52, 55, 57, 60, 79,
    80, 89, 111–113, 116, 117, 121, 125,
    134–136, 139–140, 146–147, 148,
    156–160
    See also National Election Studies;
    Primaries
Primaries, 22–23, 33, 49–52, 53–54,
63–64, 157–158, 159
Psychological theories, 15–16, 26, 27,
28, 29, 30
Public Opinion, 51
Public opinion, 22, 34, 35, 66–67, 68,
94, 109, 110, 160. *See also* Approval
ratings; Polls; Popularity
Public schools. *See* Education; School
prayer
Public service record, of candidates,
84

Quemoy, 160

Rationality, 17, 22, 25
Rationalization, 111, 116
Reader's Guide to Periodical Literature,
95
Reagan, Ronald, 1, 2, 3, 28, 29, 161,
165; extremism of, 3, 155; popularity of, 3, 63, 66, 67–70, 71, 72, 73–
91; and policy mandate, 4–11, 69–
70, 92–129, 161–162, 163–164; and
1984 election, 9, 10, 45, 50, 63, 64,
68, 71, 75, 77–78, 79, 80, 82, 83, 85,
86, 110–120, 134–135, 136, 137–139,
140, 144–146, 151, 152, 153–154,

161; and 1980 election, 10, 53, 64,
65, 68, 73, 75, 77, 82, 83, 84, 85–86,
110–118, 134–137, 139, 152, 153,
159; and primaries, 53, 56, 60, 63,
64; and choice of running mate, 59;
and personal appeal, 67–68, 69–70,
82, 83, 84, 139; and television, 68–
69; performance ratings of, 70, 71,
72, 134–155; and age, 82, 84; and
background as actor, 82, 84; and
government spending, 104, 109,
110, 112, 123–127; and civil rights,
105; and USSR, 110, 126; and tax
policy, 120, 122
Reaganomics, 56
Realignment of electorate, 2, 7–11
Refugee policy, 118
Reliability, of candidates, 81–85, 86
Republican convention. *See* Conventions
Republican Party, 37, 42–43, 46, 47,
105, 158. *See also* Parties; Republicans
Republicans, 2, 4, 9, 11, 23, 33, 39–46,
47, 48, 50, 56, 64, 65, 78, 98, 99,
100, 101, 104, 129, 131, 139, 148,
149–150, 155
Response axioms, 131
Responsible Electorate, The (Key), 8, 20,
134
Responsible party government, 160–
161, 162, 163–164
Retrospective voting, 8, 9, 132, 134, 135
Rice, Tom, 49, 50
Rivers, Douglas, 139
Robertson, Pat, 158
Rockefeller, Nelson, 52, 158
Roosevelt, Franklin D., 2, 7, 99, 143
Roosevelt, Theodore, 47, 69

Sabato, Larry, 34, 35, 40
Salamon, Lester, 4
Sandoz, Ellis, 37
Schattschneider, E. E., 93

School prayer, 119
Schroeder, Pat, 69
Schudson, Michael, 68
Secret ballot, 33
Senate candidates, 79
Shafer, Bryon, 23, 57
Shanks, J. Merrill, 94, 111, 141, 142,
144
Shefter, Martin, 7
Sigelman, Lee, 135
Size of government, 103
Smith, Al, 69
Smith, Tom, 109
Socialism, 97
Social psychology, 148
Social Sciences Citation Index, 18, 19
Social security, 8, 10, 108, 118, 119,
120, 124, 125, 127, 128
Social services spending, 5, 6, 124,
139, 141, 143, 144, 145, 146
Sociological theories, 13–15, 16, 26,
27, 28, 29, 30
South Africa, 70
Soviet Union. *See* USSR
Space, 108, 109
Spending, 5, 6, 104, 106, 107–109,
112–113, 118, 119, 120, 121, 125–
127, 128, 129, 142. *See also* Military
spending; Social services spending
State voting patterns, 36–39
Stevenson, Adlai, 24, 54, 83, 87
Stokes, Donald, 24, 92–93
Stone, Walter, 49
Strength, as candidate trait, 88–89
Survey research, 26, 130–131

Taft, Robert, 47, 48, 159
Tax policy, 5, 6–7, 10, 68, 101, 117,
118, 119, 120, 121, 122, 123, 141,
143, 158
Teapot Dome scandal, 48
Teflon-coated presidency, 69, 90
Television, 54–55, 57–58, 68–69
Tennessee, 50, 51

Terrorism, 140
Texas, 51, 156
Thurmond, Strom, 48
Ticket splitting, 36–39
Time, 164
Timex candidates, 65
Truman, Harry S, 48, 158, 159
Tweed, Boss William, 33

Udall, Morris, 55
Unemployment, 5, 69, 79, 102–103,
    106, 112, 135, 137, 138, 139, 143
United Press International (UPI), 54
University of Michigan, Survey Re-
    search Center, 15; CPS (Center for
    Political Studies) Rolling Cross-
    Section Survey, 64. *See also* Na-
    tional Election Studies
Urban Institute, 4
Urban unrest, 101
USSR, 110, 112–113, 114, 115, 119,
    126, 127, 139, 140, 141, 142, 144,
    145

Verba, Sidney, 41
Vice presidential nomination, 59–60

Vietnam War, 101, 109
Viguerie, Richard, 95
Virginia, 51
Voter Decides, The (Campbell, Gurin,
    and Miller), 15
Voting (Berelson, Lazarsfeld, and
    McPhee), 14, 17, 18, 19, 20
Voting theories, 13–30

Wages, 137, 138, 140
Wallace, George, 48, 76
War, 110, 141. *See also* Vietnam War
Watergate scandal, 148
Welfare, 108, 109, 119, 121, 143
West Virginia, 54, 157
White, Theodore, 158
Wildavsky, Aaron, 59
Williams, Philip, 34
Wilson, Woodrow, 47
Wirthlin, Richard, 4
Wisconsin, 51, 157
Women's issues, 102–103, 105, 112–
    113, 116, 117, 118, 119
Women's liberation movement, 105

Zaller, John, 131